2003

THE DUCHESS WHO WOULDN'T SIT DOWN

THE DUCHESS WHO WOULDN'T SIT DOWN

AN INFORMAL HISTORY OF HOSPITALITY

JESSE BROWNER

BLOOMSBURY

Published by Bloomsbury, New York and London
Distributed to the trade by Holtzbrinck Publishers

Library of Congress Cataloging-in-Publication Data has been applied for.

ISBN 1-58234-297-0

First U.S. Edition 2003

1 3 5 7 9 10 8 6 4 2

Typeset by Hewer Text Ltd, Edinburgh
Printed in the United States of America by
RR Donnelley & Sons, Harrisonburg, Virginia

For Cora, Sophie, and Judy

CONTENTS

INTRODUCTION

Good things are for good people; otherwise we should be reduced to the absurd belief that God created them for sinners.
Jean-Anthelme Brillat-Savarin, *The Physiology of Taste*

Not long ago, I sat down to a game of poker with five old friends. About an hour into the game, long before the heavy betting began, Guy rose from the table to help himself to a sandwich from a tray I had set out earlier. He heaped some chips onto the side of his plate, grabbed a beer from the refrigerator, and returned to his place as a hand of stud was being dealt. From the corner of my eye, I watched as he retrieved his cards with his right hand and his sandwich with his left. He studied the cards as he brought the sandwich to his mouth and bit into it. An instant later, he glanced with apparent surprise and pleasure at the sandwich, then, surreptitiously, at me. He muttered something unintelligible and sheepishly returned his gaze to the cards.

I smiled to myself. He had paid me a high, if silent, compliment. More important, though, his ill-concealed embarrassment had told me everything I needed to know about the strength of his cards. Less than a minute later, with only a pair of fours in my hand, I bluffed him out of twenty-three dollars.

I have been playing in the same floating poker game for about twelve years. Most of us went to college together, but we no longer have much in common other than our shared history and our love of poker. We were all single when the game began. Three of us are married now; some have children; some make more money than others. We often go months without seeing each other anywhere beyond the card table. The years have accentuated our differences; poker annihilates them. When I sit down on a Sunday night for six hours of card play with these men, I feel that I know them as well as I know anyone in the world. That, of course, is an illusion, but, like so much else in poker, a useful one.

The sandwiches I had prepared were no ordinary sandwiches. They had been assembled out of fresh rolls from a hundred-year-old Portuguese bakery in Connecticut; a brisket braised for more than four hours; and a horseradish sauce prepared from a secret recipe. The dish was one in a repertoire of meals I've developed specifically for poker games over the past twelve years. Cooking for card players is governed by a slew of constraints, but you can still be extremely creative and bring a delicate touch to it, if you're motivated to do so. The question is: What could possibly motivate you to do so? Why bother with such hyperactive hospitality when far less would do? It's a question I've been asking myself for a number of years.

No one could argue against the basic premise that when you cook for someone you seek to please them. It would seem self-evident that a guest's satisfaction must be the only response acceptable to an attentive host. "To entertain a guest is to make yourself responsible for his happiness so long as he is beneath your roof," says Brillat-Savarin in *The Physiology of Taste*. That sentence embodies the very essence of the traditional view of hospitality and its obligations. But of course, nothing – not even happiness – is ever as simple as it seems. Epicurus, for starters, defines two essential types of pleasure: the "moving" pleasure of fulfilling a desire and the far superior "static" pleasure of being in a state of satiety. When you eat my good food, you are happy; but when you are full of my good food, you are in a state of *ataraxia* – tranquility or serenity – that tends to overwhelm or dampen your other desires, including, perhaps, your impulse to fleece or humiliate me at the poker table.

Here is Brillat-Savarin's description of the effect of a well-prepared Barbezieux cockerel on his guests: "I saw successively imprinted on every face the glow of desire, the ecstasy of enjoyment, and the perfect calm of utter bliss" – an uncannily accurate demonstration and proof of Epicurus' thesis. Now, it goes without saying that the perfect calm of utter bliss is not a condition in which you want to be when risking the month's rent in a game of aggression, guile, and chance. So, I reasoned to myself, if my lamb-salad hero had even half the ataractic effect of the Barbezieux cockerel, I would be unbeatable.

And so it has proven. Offered in apparent generosity and selflessness – one old and trusted friend to another – my hospitality is in fact a Trojan horse, fatally compromising my rivals' defenses from within. I watch my opponents eat; they smile, they stretch, they grow chatty and convivial. They let down their guard. I strike.

What is hospitality? That would seem to be a simple question with an equally simple answer. Some four thousand years ago, an Akkadian father offered his son the following guidelines for hospitality: "Give food to eat, beer to drink, grant what is requested, provide for and treat with honor." If anyone has ever written a better or more concise summary of the host's duty, I have not read it. It is, of course, utterly delusional. Hospitality is a state of mind, not a prescriptive agenda, and defining it is an extremely vexed proposition, like asking "What is art?" or "What is good parenting?" Such questions are like the innocuous, unadorned entrance to a pyramid or a catacomb. We enter naïvely, at our own risk, and are immediately lost. Three brief, relatively straightforward visions of hospitality are more than enough to illustrate just how daunting the challenge might be:

(a) The patriarch Abraham welcomes three travelers into his tent by the oaks of Mamre. He offers them water, lamb, bread, curds, and milk and a place to rest and wash their feet. He asks nothing of them in return; requesting compensation would not be hospitable. It is enough for Abraham that strangers require food and water and that he is able and willing to provide it. That has always been the accepted version of hospitality, extended for its own sake and without ulterior motive, except perhaps for the reasonable hope that it will be extended in kind to you when you need it. But it becomes an entirely different story, with an entirely different moral, when you know that Abraham recognized the travelers as angels *before* he invited them in. Abraham's hospitality, it seems, was little more than an insurance policy.

(b) William McKay, played by Buster Keaton in *Our Hospitality*, returns to the home of his youth to claim his inheritance. A stranger in town, he is taken in by the wealthy Canfields, who offer him food, clean clothing, and a room, simply because he is in need – the very epitome of Southern hospitality. But when the Canfields discover he is a McKay, a member of the clan with which they have fought a generations-old feud, their only thought is to get him out of their house as fast as possible. Why? Because they cannot bear having an enemy under their own roof? No, it is because the rules of hospitality – which they, as honorable Southern gentlemen, must obey to the letter – require the host to ensure that no harm comes to his guest.

They can gun him down mercilessly the moment he crosses the threshold, but they are too well bred to ask him to leave. McKay, naturally enough, opts to stay. For the hosts, all the vaunted splendor of Southern hospitality boils down to nothing but a single, insuperable barrier to their desire; to the guest, it is a Chinese finger cuff, binding him tighter to his foes the more he seeks to flee them.

(c) Anyone who has ever studied accounting knows that hospitality is cited as a "specific threat" to the independence of auditors. To an auditor, enjoying a simple meal or a weekend in the country in the wrong circumstances has become more perilous to his or her reputation, credibility, and livelihood than cooking the books, lying to shareholders, or taking employment with the federal government.

Insurance, straitjacket, specific threat – we have come a long, long way from Akkadia.

Once when I was a little boy, I was out to dinner with my father when I innocently expressed sympathy for a solitary diner who, it seemed to me, looked a bit lonely eating all by himself. My father, who traveled frequently and often found himself alone in distant cities, instantly bristled at the suggestion. Some people like to eat alone, he grumbled. Why should anyone eating alone automatically be assumed to be lonely? In fact, he proposed, the best way to enjoy a good meal is alone and undistracted by chitchat and other interruptions.

My father was sorely mistaken. Eating, and hospitality in general, is a communion, and any meal worth attending by yourself is improved by the multiples of those with whom it is shared. Animals eat alone, but even then not always. The first thing monkeys did when they became humans was to gather around the campfire to celebrate, perhaps a little prematurely.

Nearly two thousand years ago, Athenaeus of Naucratis, in his *Deipnosophistae*, explicitly equated solitary eaters with criminals ("solitary eater and housebreaker!"), and just this year, the historian Felipe Fernández-Armesto, in *Near a Thousand Tables*, echoed Athenaeus' condemnation almost word for word: "that public enemy, the solitary eater." The fact is, eating in groups – along with speech, writing, and warfare – is among the most elemental and universal expressions of humanity.

But what are we to do when providing or accepting hospitality – be it a meal or a place to stay for the night – is equally fraught with ethical and pragmatic pitfalls? How do we reconcile the facts that we are incomplete alone and compromised in company? This is not, of course, a question limited to the manifestations of hospitality, but hospitality is an ideal medium for cultivating its nuances. The history of hospitality records its protagonists, from Gertrude Stein to the Emperor Nero, from Alaric the Goth to John James Audubon, at the moment when they come face to face with this paradox, unwittingly or by design. Each acquits himself or herself with varying degrees of ingenuity and self-deception, but none comes any closer than I have to resolving it. The best we can do, probably, is to return to Epicurus.

Epicurus reminds us that "the end of all our actions is to be free from pain and fear." Whatever we may do, he says – including giving pleasure to others – we ultimately do to please ourselves, and even friendship is only the most important of those means "which wisdom acquires to ensure happiness throughout the whole of life." This is not about selfishness; it is the realistic and necessary starting point of a journey on which we must seek to divest ourselves of the unnatural desires that make us unhappy. If we are lucky or persistent enough to achieve an understanding of desires whose pursuit brings us nothing but frustration, bitterness, and self-doubt, we can perhaps hope to eliminate them. The philosophy of Epicurus is not about achieving happiness through self-indulgence, as many imagine; it is about recognizing that almost all the pain and fear of our lives are based on seeking that which is not good for us. Happiness comes neither by gratifying nor by denying our desires, but by excising them. We are all doomed to seek our own happiness; we can't help ourselves. We are all, the cruel and the gentle alike, condemned to seeking that happiness in the dark. We use our need as the blind use a walking stick, to determine the safety of every forward step. We must seek instead to know what we really want – and why we want it – and stop fooling ourselves that things are good merely because we desire them.

The history of hospitality is the battlefield in which this timeless struggle with our own nature is played out in all its bloody dishonesty. It is here that we are confronted with the unspeakable truth, as inevitable as the process of natural selection and evolutionary adaptation that produced us, that we communicate with each other exclusively in a language of mutual benefits. It is here that generosity meets the pleasure principle. It is here that auditors shield themselves from their own concupiscence. It is here that refined Southern gentlemen restrain themselves from slaughtering each other. It is here that we come to understand, clearly and without flinching, Abraham's message that self-interest is the chariot of salvation. Hospitality, we'll see, is rarely about giving the guest what she needs; it is all about, and always has been about, giving the host what he needs. It is a sleight of hand whereby the host attempts to persuade the guest that she has been gratified while he reaps the far greater profit himself. Whether that profit is emotional, political, financial, or sexual is irrelevant. What is important is that hospitality be seen not as a gift, but as the transaction that it is, a trade-off so subliminal even the host may not be aware it has taken place, or of the ways in which it has profited him.

Since common wisdom generally ranks hospitality among the cardinal virtues – right alongside charity, mercy, self-sacrifice, loyalty, and temperance – this is a lesson that most of us will tend to resist and that cannot be learned frivolously. That is why I have chosen to deliver it in reverse chronological order in this book, easing us backward through time as a sleeper gradually descends into the realm of dreams, where demons that ought not be approached too abruptly may await. It is also why I have deliberately limited my scope of inquiry to Western civilization: just as I have never learned anything of much interest in my dreams about anyone other than myself, so too I deemed it wise to stick to what I have at least a chance at understanding.

I labored under years of self-deception to recognize and acknowledge the subversive power of my poker sandwiches; before that, I had myself convinced that I was merely giving my guests a decent meal and that simple thanks were my only due reward. I can't say that I'm a better person for this self-knowledge, but at least I have laid bare the moral dilemma underlying my actions. Either I maintain my culinary standards and count my winnings, or I serve up Blimpies and lose my shirt.

CHAPTER I

HOW TO PUT YOUR GUESTS AT EASE

If such a little piece of meat, white and mild, lies in kraut, that is a picture of Venus in the roses.

Ludwig Uhland, *A Pork-Soup Song*

In 1938, the German Oberkommando der Wehrmacht published a remarkable document titled *Speisenzusammenstellung unter Mitverwedung von Edelsoja Mit Kochanweisungen* (Formulation of menus including pure soya, with recipes). It was an official German army recipe book based on recent scientific research into the value of soybeans as a viable substitute for meat. Soy was a much more efficient supplier of protein than pea meal, the principal protein supplement during the Franco-Prussian and First World Wars. The year 1918 had been a time of traumatic hunger and near starvation for Germany; clearly, in preparing for the coming war, the Oberkommando was taking no chances this time. By 1938, the hoarding of soy flour was already well underway.

What is remarkable about the recipe book is its optimism. If you didn't know that it was a military publication, you might easily mistake it for a cookbook written for the traditional German hausfrau of a prosperous provincial town. Its hundreds of unmistakably German dishes are ample, rich in protein and fat, and seasoned with some delicacy and sophistication. They include Cassel spareribs, sauerbraten, roast veal, smoked short ribs, corned beef brisket, roast mutton, roast venison, pork chops, beef roulade, pork pepperpot, veal goulash, venison stew, kidney stew, pickled tripe, hopple-popple, lung hash, goat sausage, Königsberg meatballs in caper sauce, blood sausage, fish dumplings in dill sauce and thirty hot soups – all supplemented with rather than replaced by soy – along with fifteen sweet soups, two dozen sauces and gravies, twenty salads, and a variety of tempting desserts. How many, if any, of these actually made their way into Wehrmacht bellies I do not know, and in any case no soldier in any army, conscript or volunteer, qualifies as a guest. Still, if he was offered even one meal in ten from the *Speisenzusammenstellung unter Mitverwedung*, he must have felt right at home and well primed for action, not to mention patriotic. He certainly couldn't count on being fed half so well in Poland.

The first object of any host must be to put his guests at their ease. From the moment they step through the door, they should want to be precisely where they are and nowhere else. If they are not relaxed, comfortable, and suggestible, all a host's other hard work cooking, making seating assignments, or rearranging the guest room will have been futile. This may seem like a perfectly obvious point, but it is one that is neither automatic nor easy.

There's always an edge of trepidation and discomfort in standing on a threshold, no matter how intimate the host and the guest may believe themselves to be. The guest is entrusting herself to the host's benevolence, but we all understand instinctively that few of us even know what is in our own best interests, let alone those of a disparate group of others. In *The Rituals of Dinner*, Margaret Visser goes so far as to suggest that, ultimately, table manners evolved as a way of reassuring the guest that he would not be eaten, or at least murdered, by the host. I'm not sure that she intends for us to take this literally, but there is no doubt that, as she says, "hosts are, at least ritually and temporally, more powerful than guests." This is true for guests at a meal where the host dispenses the food, and even more so for overnight guests, who are at their most vulnerable asleep in a strange bed. We know this to be so but dismiss our ancient instincts. We are animals, but we hardly ever listen to, or even hear, what our animal natures are telling us about our immediate environment. Eating and crossing territorial boundaries are fraught with dangers and anxieties that even we civilized beasts continue to sense and respond to, although we may be only dimly conscious of them.

Unable to grasp what these instinctive feelings are saying, we translate our heightened awareness of danger into an emotional idiom that we are more familiar with. What kind of mood is the host in? Has he had another fight with his wife? Does their apartment still stink of wet dog? What will they be serving? Who else is coming? Who will I be asked to sit next to? How is my breath? Am I going to make a fool of myself? Even if the host is our oldest friend in the world, at least one of these questions or something similar will be in the back of our minds as we ring the doorbell. We may not even be aware of it, but we are edgy and waiting to be relieved of our natural anxieties.

The host must have a firm grasp of this issue and address it robustly from the outset. There is scant margin for error – if the guests' anxieties cannot be assuaged in the first three minutes after their arrival, it is unlikely that anything the host may do thereafter will fully succeed in dispelling them. This, too, is perfectly natural. We arrive expecting to be made to feel welcome, safe, and among the like-minded. When this does not happen immediately – and, as it were, organically – we cannot help but sense that something is subtly amiss. For the rest of our stay, no matter what happens, we will be on our guard, perhaps only subliminally, anticipating trouble. It's the difference between the emotional status of a predator who has killed his prey and owns it, and that of a scavenger who finds his meal laid out for him by an unknown benefactor who may return at any moment to claim it. In other words, the host's first task is to make the guest forget that she is a guest, a scavenger. Forget about fancy cooking and radish-carving; forget about rare burgundies and the perfectly caramelized tarte Tatin; forget about Frette sheets and Ralph Lauren hand towels. These assets collectively may make for a decent meal or country weekend, but it is the ability to put guests at their ease that distinguishes a good host from a great one.

Every host has his or her own way of making this happen. There is no right way, and I would never presume to offer advice. In any case, there is a multibillion-dollar industry of magazines, television channels, and pundits ever willing to take your money for their so-called expertise if you insist on believing that such knowledge can be bought. It is, of course, an alchemical equation, dependent as much on instinct as on skill and experience. I am not even sure that it is something that can be taught. Any idiot can master the rules of poker in five minutes; consistent success requires a keen eye for weakness, an exquisite grasp of human nature, and the ruthless will to exploit them to your own advantage. The same is true of hospitality. Your guests *must* be made to bend to your will or else you are lost.

The psychologists, chefs, and generals of the German Oberkommando had a fine understanding of the guest mentality. How pleased they must have been, in that fall of 1938, to stand in the mess hall doorway and watch their strapping lads tuck into their Königsberg meatballs in caper sauce, as lusty and boisterous as if they were back home at mother's kitchen table. What a grand party the next few years were going to be! How golden was the autumn sun on the vast fields of ripening soy in East Prussia and the Ukraine! Those Nazi caterers had every reason to be pleased

12

with themselves – they had learned at the feet of the greatest master of them all.

In 1922, thirty-three year-old Adolf Hitler went hiking with his friend Dietrich Eckart in the Obersalzburg, a region of bucolic pastures and Alpine peaks in southern Bavaria. On a steep slope above the town of Berchtesgaden, he was enchanted by a modest cottage, the Haus Wachenfeld, built in 1916. Hitler never forgot the discovery. Upon his release from Landsberg Prison in 1924, he returned to Berchtesgaden and rented a nearby chalet, a peaceful refuge in which to finish the second volume of *Mein Kampf*. In 1928, drawing on financing that remains murky to this day, he purchased Haus Wachenfeld and brought in his step-sister, Angela Raubal, and her daughter Geli to tend to the household. For the next seventeen years, it was to remain his favorite home, a cherished retreat, the place to which he planned to retire after he had completed his monumental mission. It was also his favored venue for personal and official hospitality, invitations to which were coveted and eagerly sought by the Nazi elite, members of the international diplomatic corps, and journalists.

By 1933, the chalet had been extensively rebuilt and renamed Berghof – "mountain court." Surrounding farms were annexed, either by purchase or coercion, to ensure Hitler's privacy. Eventually, Rudolf Hess fenced the compound to keep the growing hordes of Hitler's idolizers at arm's length. It ultimately incorporated some ten square kilometers, including homes for the Görings and the Goebbelses, SS barracks, the luxurious Platterhof hotel, civil service offices, and a vast underground network of bunkers outfitted with inlaid floors, wainscoting, bathrooms, kitchens, and kennels. The Eagle's Nest, a teahouse built for the führer by Martin Bormann on the fifty-five-hundred-foot Kehlstein, was accessible only by a tortuous five-mile road lined with machine-gun nests, leading through a 170-yard tunnel to a two-hundred-foot elevator shaft blasted into the stone and fitted with hidden poison-gas nozzles. The entire compound was protected against air raids by giant smoke machines that could shroud it in dense fog at a moment's notice. It was to this place, his country home, that Hitler yearned to flee whenever the pressures of Berlin grew too burdensome.

The Berghof itself was designed as an official residence. Its most famous feature was the imposing conference hall, with its hardwood coffering and an enormous picture window that could be lowered into the floor at the flick of a switch to turn the great room into a covered veranda. The hall was provided with Biedermeier and baroque furnishings, Persian carpets, and an ornate Bechstein piano and decorated with paintings and tapestries, one of which concealed a large movie screen. There was a well-appointed dining room, paneled in cembra pine, with a table that sat twenty-four and a more intimate breakfast nook. There was Hitler's personal library, from which guests were free to borrow. There was a lovely winter garden enclosed in glass and terraces with sweeping views. The basement held a bowling alley. Upstairs was Hitler's private study, equipped with electric alarms on every door and canisters of tear gas that the führer could release at the press of a button. Sleeping quarters were available for members of the household and guests. Hitler's modest bedroom connected to Eva Braun's via a bathroom that was hidden from view to maintain decorum. Every guest room had a copy of *Mein Kampf* and French pornographic books at the bedside.

Very few aspirants ever made it through the gates of the Berghof complex. Wealthy industrialists and well-connected party officials might be lucky enough to rank a stay at the pricey Platterhof – originally conceived as a low-cost "people's hotel" for ordinary Germans seeking the thrill of proximity with their führer – but only the most exalted elite ever enjoyed access to the Berghof proper, let alone a room for the night. Still, there was no mistaking the fact that, once in, you were a private guest in Hitler's home, and Hitler prided himself on his hospitality. An invitation to the Berghof was the ultimate billet-doux in the Third Reich.

Many readers may find it distasteful that a writer should undertake an assessment of Hitler based solely on his abilities as a private host. And yet, because we all have a tendency to give what we most want to receive, a person is likely to be at his most self-revealing when he is acting as a host. Our gifts are models of our own desires. It is not that, in slaving away all day on an immaculate chicken potpie or authentic cassoulet, I am telling my guests that I expect them to work just as hard when I come to their house. It is not that, in bringing strangers together who will go on to form lasting friendships, I am expressing unspoken disappointment in the friends I already have. Nor, in opening my doors to foreign travelers, am I signaling my intention of descending upon them one day in an unbridled orgy of reciprocation. What I *am* offering is a privileged peek into my psyche. I am saying: "This is my vision of a perfect world. This magnificent chicken potpie, this charming Ivy League professor, these fragrant sheets of Egyptian cotton – all produced for your pleasure without any apparent effort on my part – are the shibboleths of my desire. I have worked so hard for so long; the things I want, the respect that is my due, the love I crave should fall to me now without toil. I deserve to be a guest in my own life." An observant guest can learn an awful lot about her host from what he offers.

This is especially true of Hitler because, although consumed at all times with affairs of state, even while at the Berghof, he prided himself on being a gracious and attentive host, offering his guests what he believed they wanted while controlling every aspect of their stay under his roof. The extension of hospitality was for Hitler, as it is for us all, an unparalleled opportunity to model utopia, the world as it would be if we were in full control of our environment and company. What you can never learn about Hitler the politician, Hitler the military strategist, Hitler the genocidal monster, you can be sure to learn about Hitler the affable host.

Guests at the Berghof lived according to the host's schedule. They tiptoed around the house while the führer slept in, often until noon. They bided their time until lunch while he worked in camera with his military and political advisers. Hitler would then appear, leading his guests in procession to the dining room, where the table had been set with Rosenthal porcelain (or solid silver for important guests) and the place settings meticulously inspected by the host himself. After lunch, Hitler led a walking party to the teahouse – not the Eagle's Nest but one just up the hill through the woods – where tea and cakes were served. If the führer happened to doze off there, the guests would rush outside for a smoke. After his official nap back at the Berghof, Hitler returned to work, leaving the guests to their own devices. Supper was at eight; the ladies wore evening dresses, the men wore uniforms, and the SS waiters wore white jackets. After supper, he worked again, often until midnight, but the guests were now required to wait for him in the conference hall. When their leader finally joined them, they might settle in for a late-night movie, following which they could expect him to indulge in lengthy monologues on a variety of subjects, some extending to several hours. Hitler drank hot chocolate with whipped cream while his guests took coffee or brandy. Those who could slipped away to the terrace for a smoke, but they were called back when their absence was noticed. Some time around four or five in the morning the führer finally wore himself down and went off to bed, leaving the guests free to smoke and drink at their leisure.

Very few guests, with the possible exception of some official spouses, were compelled against their will to attend upon the führer. Grouse as they might about the restraints and enforced idleness, they were all there because they had actively petitioned to be there, and for every invitee who might be asked up for the last time, there were tens of thousands waiting to take his place. To that extent, Hitler had no need to extend the graces of a traditional host. Simply by allowing them into his presence he was giving them precisely what they sought. If you were stupid enough to offend the host – as Henriette von Schirach learned after she deplored the plight of Jewish refugees she had seen in Holland – you risked being summarily banished by an adjutant ("You have made him very angry. Please leave at once!"), but you really had no one to blame but yourself.

And yet, by all accounts, Hitler could be the very model of charm and graciousness when he chose to. Many were the guests who, having driven up the steep and often icy road from Berchtesgaden and past the forbidding SS barracks, were amazed to find the führer himself awaiting them at the head of the Berghof stairs. He was always concerned with their health and ready with medical and nutritional advice. And while he neither smoked nor drank, and was never too tired to launch into a numbing diatribe against these vices, he had a ready supply of beer, wine, and liquor for his guests and tolerated their smoking on the terraces. Only Eva Braun felt it strictly necessary to pop a breath mint before slipping back inside. Hitler clearly saw himself as a congenial and tolerant man, his hospitality reflecting his vision of an Aryan society so ethnically pure that it could afford to indulge a few, relatively harmless vices. The Berghof was his prototype for postwar Germany, and his hospitality the model of the tolerant system by which it would be governed.

This "tolerance" is most tellingly highlighted by his attitude toward meat and meat-eating. If you run the words "Hitler" and "vegetarian" through an Internet search engine, you will find any number of essays by prominent vegetarian intellectuals denying that Hitler was one of theirs. Their principal argument seems to be that, because Hitler may not have been a perfect vegetarian, he was not one at all. In fact, all of the evidence points to his having been a committed vegetarian and a vocal defender of vegetarianism. Joseph Goebbels in his diary records several pro-vegetarian rants, while Doctor Theodor Morell, Hitler's personal physician, who spent an inordinate amount of time recording his patient's eating habits and analyzing his bowel movements, never once indicates the presence of any meat in his diet and explicitly calls him a vegetarian. It is true that Hitler came to vegetarianism gradually, only slowly losing his taste for liver dumplings, but after the 1931 suicide of his beloved niece and paramour Geli Raubal, he seems to have abandoned meat-eating altogether. "It is like eating a corpse!" he said of his breakfast ham the day after her death. The famous 1936 photo of Hitler sharing a meat-laden *Eintopf* with Goebbels at the Chancellery in Berlin has been identified as having been posed for propaganda purposes.

In fact, there had been a venerable association in Germany between vegetarianism, anti-Semitism, and virulent nationalism since the mid-nineteenth century. Gustav von Struve and Richard Wagner were both passionate animal-rights activists whose "sympathy with all that lives" did not extend to Jews. Goebbels, Hermann Göring, and Heinrich Himmler were all dedicated to advancing animal rights. As Master of the German Hunt, Göring tightened laws on hunting, restocked forests, prohibited vivisection, and banned cruel hunting practices. "He who tortures animals wounds the feelings of the German people," he insisted with touching empathy. Hitler, of course, was an ardent admirer of Wagner and subscribed to his theory that human migration northward had led to "that thirst [for flesh and blood] which history teaches us can never be slaked, and fills its victims with a raging madness, not with courage." This was the kind of paradox with which Hitler was apparently comfortable; another was his conviction that meat-eating caused chronic constipation and flatulence, from which he nevertheless suffered mightily throughout his vegetarian years. "After eating a vegetable plat-ter," Morell noted of Hitler in his dairy, "constipation and colossal flatulence occurred on a scale I have seldom encountered before."

I also happen to believe – admittedly without direct evidence – that Hitler at some point fell under the influence of the renowned Swiss nutritionist Dr. Max Bircher-Benner, the inventor of muesli. Hitler's view that energy came from a vegetarian diet, that "meat-eating is harmful to humanity," and that "much of the decay of our civilization [can be attributed] to meat-eating" largely parallels Bircher-Benner's theory that "All kinds of meat, as well as fish and poultry, bring about a slow decay of the vital tissues of the human organism," and that "MEAT THEREFORE DOES NOT GIVE STRENGTH." The 1934 cookbook of "health-giving dishes" served at Bircher-Benner's sanatorium lists innumerable recipes known to be among Hitler's favorites. Despite almost relentless epigastric pain, Hitler ate a great deal of raw vegetables, a practice highly endorsed by Bircher-Benner. In view of their mutual obsession with "poisoning of the juices," it is easy to see how theories on the purity of body and the purity of blood were conflated. It is no coincidence that, under a vegetarian dictator, the National Health Department adopted as its slogan "The wholesome life is a national duty."

Like ideologues of every stripe, militant vegetarians can be as judgmentally superior and as absolutist in their rejection of relative values as any ayatollah. One might therefore be forgiven for expecting a brutal Nazi megalomaniacal vegetarian despot to exploit his powers to enforce his views, especially to the benefit of the entire *Volk*. In fact, Hitler did nothing of the kind. He was remarkably forbearing and accommodating with meat-eaters, who naturally made up the majority of his guests. At the Chancellery and at the Berghof, there were always two menus, one vegetarian, the other not, served with mineral water, beer, and wine.

In *The Vegetable Passion: A History of the Vegetarian State of Mind*, Janet Barkas quotes from Berghof menu cards that she obtained from a privileged source. The meals, hardly haute cuisine, seem to have been quite typical of both dining rooms:

July 13, 1937
   Consommé with marrow dumplings
   Stuffed peppers
   Home-fried potatoes
   Green salad
Vegetarian:
   Soup
   Noodles with cream of wheat
   Green salad
   Cheese – Fruit

July 14, 1937 (Lunch)
   Potato soup
   Baked fish
   Stuffed breast of veal
   Potatoes
   Mixed salad

Vegetarian:
Consommé with noodles
Baked squash
Potato salad
Filling made of rolls
Salad
Fruit tarts

July 14, 1937 (Dinner)
Asparagus soup
Potato puffer
Cranberries
Mixed cold cuts
Cheese – fruit

Vegetarian:
Consommé with noodles
Home-fried dumplings made of rolls
Green salad or potato puffer
Applesauce

Hitler often did lecture his guests on the evils of meat-eating, once turning the stomachs of an entire audience with his description of a slaughterhouse he had visited in the Ukraine. At mealtimes, however, he did not pressure them to follow his example, though many apparently abstained from meat-eating in his presence, only to later retire to another room to gorge on flesh out of his sight. It is not at all clear that such sycophancy was warranted. In her memoirs, Göring's wife Emmy relates a 1933 visit to the Berghof at which she made her distaste for vegetarianism apparent to the führer:

"It looks to me as though you would prefer a good steak."

"I certainly would," I said. "I can not understand how you can get enough to eat just from all these vegetables."

Everyone around the table looked at me reproachfully and shocked. It was as though I had committed a crime of *lèse majesté*, for all the others were silently eating their raw vegetables.

"Bring Frau Sonnemann a large beef steak," said Adolf Hitler to the butler.

"And one for me too," Hermann called out, "and above all a glass of beer."

Hitler laughed heartily. From then on I was given both at mid-day and in the evenings such an enormous steak that I could hardly manage it.

At the Berghof, Hitler himself did not partake of these meals. Instead, he ate dishes prepared exclusively from fruits and vegetables grown in Martin Bormann's model garden and greenhouses. His tastes in food hovered somewhere between the mundane and the revolting. All historians seem to agree that he had an inordinate passion for oatmeal gruel and linseed oil, which he doused liberally over his orange juice, baked potatoes, and cottage cheese. He was also fond of pea soup – which, served up as "Hindenburg grenades" during the First World War, must have been his madeleine, recalling his happiest days in the trenches – but dared not eat it because of his flatulence. Dr. Morell recalls Hitler being served "pickles without meat, all mashed up, but he doesn't feel like trying it yet, so it was stuffed empanadillos (Pfannkuchen-Taschen) with pureed carrots and mashed potatoes, rounded off with strawberries." According to Janet Barkas, his favorite dishes included asparagus tips and artichoke hearts in cream sauce. He also liked eggs, fried or boiled with mayonnaise, and rice pudding with herb sauce. Dessert was often an apple, stewed, baked, or in cake, or a slice of gooseberry pie. He never inflicted these preferences on his guests, for which they must have been truly grateful.

Like any good host, Hitler knew his guests and what they would and would not tolerate, even from him. It was one thing to exhort, cajole, berate, and generally infantilize a nation of faceless worshippers; quite another to try it on his private guests, close personal associates who knew him far too well already. The last thing he wanted was to read their intimate opinion of him – a ruthless dictator who ate baby food; a bloodthirsty vegetarian; a commander of armies who looked at his breakfast and saw his lover's corpse – reflected in their eyes across the dining room table. The fear of being "recognized" may have been another source of his tolerance of meat-eaters in his own home when he was so intolerant of deviance in any other sphere.

He had a reasonably realistic sense of his own limitations in another way, too. The Berghof was hard to reach, often frozen in, and comparatively modest in its fare and amenities. There is a limit, after all, to how often you can ask visiting statesmen to go bowling. Even had he wanted to offer something more, and saucier, his public image as the chaste, faithful, and eremitic bridegroom of the German people would never have permitted the least suggestion of decadence. When such decadence was called for, when he needed something more to impress and sweet-talk a foreign dignitary, Hitler turned to his Reichsmarschall and designated successor, Hermann Göring. In the game of Nazi hospitality, Göring was Hitler's alter-ego, Mr. Hyde to Hitler's Dr. Jekyll, with license to deploy the kind of opulence and excess that the führer could never be seen to condone. In fact, Hitler not only sanctioned Göring's behavior, but also promoted it as an extension of his own hospitality into forbidden territory.

Göring's "hunting lodge," Karinhall, stood some eighty-five kilometers northeast of Berlin in Schorfheide. Like the Berghof, Karinhall was a private residence converted at state expense into a semiofficial Nazi entertainment hall. When Hitler needed to soften up staunch adversaries or potential allies, he sent them to Göring, who often received guests in flamboyant silk robes or a full leather suit, his lips apparently painted and cheeks rouged. The front entrance was hung with massive oaken doors, like something out of *The Hobbit*. The dining hall was finished in white marble and hung with Gobelins tapestries. The house had its own cinema and the best Berlin caterer, Horcher, at its disposal. At least three notables – the Duke of Windsor, Charles Lindbergh, and Japanese foreign minister Yosuke Matsuoka – were treated to a delightful day playing with Göring's spectacular model train set, with salutary results for Nazi foreign policy.

Unlike Hitler, Göring's tastes in catering ran to the excessive. His marriage to Emmy Sonnemann in 1935 included a seventy-five-plane flyover, a gala performance of *Lohengrin*, and a wedding breakfast at the Hotel Kaiserhof for 316 at which lobster, turtle soup, turbot, pâté de foie gras, roast chicken, ices, and Welsh rarebit were served. For his party to celebrate the 1936 Olympics, Göring transformed the gardens of his palace on the Leipziger Platz into "a sort of Oktoberfest beer garden, with a fairground in the middle, helle and dunkel beer on tap (as well as champagne and liquors), sausages, roast game, corn on the cob, and mounds of potatoes and sauerkraut," according to historian Leonard Mosley. The guests were entertained with performances by the principal dancers and corps de ballet of the Berlin Opera and were later assembled on the lawns to enjoy an aerobatics display by the famed pilot Ernst Udet. The party broke up shortly before dawn.

On January 12, 1945, Göring threw a lavish, desperate last party at Karinhall. "This is no time to deny ourselves," he said.

"We will all be getting a *Genickschuss* (a shot in the neck) very soon now." While most Germans were scrambling for scraps, Göring's guests were treated to "caviar from Russia, duck and venison from the Schorfheide forests, Danzig salmon and the last of the French pâté de foie gras." They also enjoyed "100 bottles of French Champagne, 180 bottles of vintage wines, eighty-five bottles of French Cognac, fifty bottles of imported liqueurs, 500 imported cigars and 4,000 cigarettes." Occupying American troops found twenty-five thousand bottles of champagne in the wine cellar of his home in Berchtesgaden the following May.

Back at the Berghof, by January 1945 – with certain defeat in sight and Germany's cities already in smoldering ruins – the hospitality situation had deteriorated dramatically. As we have seen, at the height of his powers Hitler had a keen grasp of just how useful the subtle indulgence could be to a host's reputation and his guests' morale. Now, however, with his grip on reality fatally loosened, his hosting instincts were correspondingly dulled. He pared down the menu, serving spaghetti with ketchup, mushrooms, and curds, and decreed the Sunday meal to be *Eintopfgericht* – leftovers served from a single pot. *Eintopf* was now represented by the state media as a "national meal of communitarian sacrifice and solidarity." Not surprisingly, guests stopped accepting invitations to the Berghof and he took to eating alone, the last refuge of a desperate man and, as I have indicated elsewhere, a clear indication of criminality.

There is some anecdotal evidence to support the claim that Hitler had intended to address the problem of German meat-eating after his victory in the war. Goebbels explicitly refers to this plan in his diary entry of April 26, 1942: "Of course he knows that during the war we cannot completely upset our food system. After the war, however, he intends to tackle this problem also." He needn't have worried – by 1942, Germany was well on its way to becoming vegetarian by default. Although a German soldier's meat ration was three times that of a civilian's, it is safe to say that Cassel spareribs and roast venison were no longer on the menu.

Watching German diners stuff themselves on sole and duck at the Tour d'Argent in occupied Paris in 1942, Ernst Jünger noted, "In times like these, to eat well and to eat a lot gives a feeling of power." That may have been of some consolation to those on the homefront – who had been told "they have to go without food so that the starving people of Europe may be fed" – but I doubt it. By that time, they were drinking antifreeze or paying one hundred marks per pound for black-market tea. On April 22, 1942, the Nazi mouthpiece *Völkischer Beobachter* announced, "Less food will be offered, according to the simpler way of life introduced for the nation and a rationed cuisine . . . There are two meatless days a week." In June, the *Westdeutscher Beobachter* editorialized, "Caterers must compensate for small meat portions with larger portions of potatoes, vegetables or salads." Coupons for hotel meals were assessed down to the tiniest allotment of nutrition, "even as to how much fat is to be used for a certain dish and how much flour for thickening the sauce."

The use of the word "ersatz" was forbidden; the patriotic euphemism "German" was endorsed for synthetic products, as in the joke "Germans buy German Van Goghs." But by then the quality of even these supplements was so awful that on April 24 the *Deutsche Volkswirt* was forced to announce, "Expressions like 'German' pepper, 'German' caviare are forbidden from now on because they are apt to injure the good reputation of German products in general." The ersatz "new flour" with which wartime bread was made was so hazardous to the public's health that eating it fresh could make a person sick; it had to be allowed to mature for several days before it was safe to eat. Heinz Pfennig, a

German lieutenant at Stalingrad, lived on dried potato flakes. His rations for Christmas Day 1942 were one tablespoon of peas, two tablespoons of potato soup, and two squares of chocolate. No soy. This was a diet that even the führer himself might have enjoyed.

Needless to say, things were even worse by the end of the war. In 1946, civilians in occupied Germany were on starvation rations that could be as low as one thousand calories per day; by the next year, the official ration in the French sector was down to four hundred and fifty calories per day, half that of the Belsen concentration camp. Meat, it is to be assumed, was not a part of the ration.

Hitler had managed to turn Germany into a nation of vegetarians after all. The vegetarianism that he had been unwilling to enforce in his role as the host of the Berghof was now the national practice. And, as Janet Barkas points out, it was roughly compatible with kosher dietary restrictions.

CHAPTER II

TEDDY BEARS' PICNIC

But your passion is a lie . . . It isn't passion at all, it is your will. It's your bullying will. You want to clutch things and have them in your power. You want to have things in your power. And why? Because you haven't got any real body, any dark sensual body of life. You have no sensuality. You have only your will and your conceit of consciousness, and your lust for power, to know.

D. H. Lawrence, *Women in Love*

Once we have put our guests at their ease, another basic element essential to successful hospitality, at once apparently simple and treacherously subtle, is the ability to make them feel special. Each and every invitee should be made to feel that he or she has been included for reasons that are unique and particular and sought out for the singular contribution that he or she is able to make to the gathering. This is true even if we have only invited our inner circle of intimate friends; their egos, too, need petting and will not be satisfied to imagine that the requirement of their presence is based on pure sentiment, since being liked for the wrong reasons can be as enervating as being disliked. Let them suffer the torments of hell when they are alone with their insecurities and free-floating anxieties; at our house, they are members of a charmed circle, a privileged fellowship of exalted individuals.

The problem is, few of us know enough exalted individuals to make up the guest list of even one dinner party, let alone an entire season's worth. And even if we did, a roomful of exalted individuals can be tiresome, loud, and competitive, like an orchestra made up exclusively of trumpets. Those who are more exalted, or consider themselves to be more exalted, may make those who are less exalted, or fear themselves to be less exalted, feel inadequate; the less exalted will be quick – and rightly so – to blame the host for their unfortunate condition. And a dinner attended by a hive of angry, more or less exalted individuals is not likely to prove a success.

And so, as always, the host is called on to be manipulative, sly, and duplicitous – in other words, creative. After all, the party does not put itself together. Everything, including and especially a guest's sense of his own worth, is the host's responsibility. If two guests fail to see eye to eye, or a visitor's hypersensitive back goes into spasm after a night on the sofa bed, that, too, is nobody's fault but the host's. The trick, as always, is to ensure that the balance of power remains firmly tilted to the host's side. What every host would do well to keep in mind is that people are generally only too happy to find a dominant force to surrender to. When a host is fully in control of every aspect of her hospitality, and when she exerts that control with skill, tact, and sensitivity, she can be confident that her guests will deliver themselves willingly, gratefully, into her serene authority.

My five-year-old daughter, Cora, displays an instinctive grasp of this challenge every time she holds a tea party for her dolls and teddy bears. She has a great many dolls and teddy bears, but only a select few are invited to any given entertainment. She compiles her list with such exquisite discrimination that the guests rarely quarrel or complain; when they do, she steps in between them and knows just what to say to smooth their ruffled fur. She seats them just so and after great deliberation. Only she is permitted to serve the tea and cakes. She speaks for each in turn and the conversation is always fluid and enlightened. She also knows just when to call it a night so that everyone leaves with the unspoiled impression of having enjoyed a delightful tea among a group of clever and amiable peers.

Regrettably, you cannot treat your guests as if they were teddy bears. They tend to be self-centered, obtuse, and vituperative in ways that stuffed animals seldom are, and they will know it if we try openly to patronize them. But if, like most hosts, we secretly hope to be lavished with compliments and extolled for our virtue and wisdom, there is a way to get our guests to cooperate. It requires the resolve, patience, and determination to make them utterly dependent on our benevolence. Then they will fall in line like so many teddy bears. If we are clear about our priorities, and if we approach them just right, we can treat our guests just like our favorite toys, and they will reward us in ways that we – adults long since resigned to complex relationships of scant emotional immediacy – can scarcely allow ourselves to hope for. They may not love us unconditionally, admire us, praise us, pet us, hug and kiss us, or cling to us through the long, lonely night, as we might wish they would, but they will assume all of our pains and fears as their own, and they will never betray us.

In the early twentieth century, there lived two women, born within a year of each other, who were internationally famous for their hospitality during their own lifetimes. Each tried in her own way to make teddy bears of her guests, to line them up into a chorus of mouthpieces, and each needed more from her guests than she was willing or able to ask for directly. One may be said to have succeeded in all of her hopes and ambitions; the other, to have failed miserably. Their strangely parallel lives demonstrate the risks and rewards of hosting a teddy bears' picnic.

*　　　*　　　*

Lady Ottoline Violet Anne Cavendish Bentinck (1873–1938) was a sad and lonely child. Half-sister to the sixth duke of Portland and youngest sibling to four considerably older brothers who had little interest in her, she was raised at the family seat of Welbeck, Nottinghamshire, following the death of her beloved father when she was four. The fifth duke had been a notorious eccentric who had excavated miles of tunnels and ballrooms under the castle and decorated most of the rooms in pink and gold, with no furniture but an open commode in the corner of each. One chamber, eerily, was stockpiled floor-to-ceiling with brown wigs in green boxes. The kitchen was located in an outbuilding and meals were sent to the house on heated trucks via underground rail. Her mother was sickly and protective; her only adult friend, the duke's librarian, was sent away for smoking in the dining room. Ottoline spent a great deal of time alone in her room, which she divided in two with a curtain. She slept on one side of the curtain; on the other, she staged dramatic performances with her dolls, to which no one came.

She grew into an awkward and pious teenager, horse-faced, six feet tall, and with hair the color of marmalade. She was already suffering the headaches that were to plague her for the rest of her life. Her favorite reading was Thomas à Kempis's *The Imitation of Christ*. She held Bible classes for the farmhands in her spare time. Her first mentor and heroine was the reclusive Mother Julian. Dancing lessons in London proved a dismal failure, for she was too shy to dance. She was sixteen when her brother the duke – to whom she referred exclusively as "Portland" – married, and she and her ailing mother retired to a family house in Chertsey, Surrey. Ottoline spent the next three years nursing the dying woman, the drear monotony broken only by a disastrous coming-out. A short trip to Italy was followed by her mother's death, upon which she was shipped off to her brother's house in Langwell,

Scotland, where she was assiduously shunned by his hunting companions.

Ottoline couldn't help but know that she was different from others of her class. Throughout her twenties, she vainly sought a means of escape, with the sole aim of avoiding being forced into marriage with one of her brother's friends. She tried studying, at Edinburgh and Oxford, but found herself unsuited to academics. She tried travel; her second voyage to Italy, accompanied by a dour governess, was enlivened by a brief passion for the charismatic psychologist Axel Munthe, a man twice her age. His offer of a guest cottage on his estate in Anacapri was made at a price she was unwilling to pay, however, and he dismissed her by noting that he already had enough neurotics in his practice and did not need one at home. Until she met the Oxford lawyer Philip Morrell, it seemed as if the life she aspired to – vaporously envisioned as one "lived on the same plane as poetry and as music" – was going to be beyond her grasp.

They were married in 1902, the same year in which Philip alienated both his and her families by running as a Liberal for a seat in Parliament; he alienated them even further by winning. Lady Ottoline Morrell was now a politician's wife, a step up from her former abjectness but not quite what she was looking for. In 1905, Philip opened a practice in London. They took a house at 44 Bedford Square, in the Bloomsbury neighborhood just then rising to respectability as an enclave of fashionable intellectualism. In 1906, Ottoline gave birth to the twins Hugh and Julian (a girl); Hugh died of a brain hemorrhage three days later, and a subsequent operation left Ottoline unable to bear more children. Strangely, of all her life's watersheds, it was this tragedy that galvanized her to remake herself in the image that had by then taken hold of her imagination. Declaring in 1907 that "I am not suited to good works," she decided "to launch recklessly on the sea of London." The makeover was comprehensive, to say the least.

At first, her guest list drew heavily on Philip's liberal and political connections and on her Bloomsbury neighbors. Henry James, Bertrand Russell, and Prime Minister Herbert Henry Asquith were among the early regulars. Lady Ottoline soon found that she had the instincts of a born hostess. "I was intensely interested in these people – most of whom were remarkable in some way and I who found them so exciting, so thrilling, was anxious that they should know each other. If I liked a personality my instinct was that I wanted that one to meet others in whom I was interested."

Within a year, her Thursday evening "at homes" for artists, writers, politicians, and intellectuals had become the preeminent salon of London and 44 Bedford Square "the most civilised few hundred square feet in the world." Virginia Stephen (later Woolf) wrote: "We have just got to know a wonderful Lady Ottoline Morrell, who has the head of a Medusa; but she is very simple & innocent in spite of it, & worships the arts." Quentin Bell found her "extremely simple and not very clever," but conceded that "she brought petticoats, frivolity and champagne to the buns, the buggery and high thinking of Fitzroy Square."

Now considered to be striking rather than awkward, she welcomed her guests from the balcony of the second-floor landing, done up in Grecian, Cossack, or Oriental dress. In one of the more generous descriptions of her newfound flamboyance, Virginia Stephen likened her to a Spanish galleon, "hung with golden coins, & lovely silken sails." A typical costume was one described by Vanessa Bell: "It might have been designed by Bakst for a Russian ballet on a Circassian folktale theme. Russian boots of red morocco were revealed under a full, light-blue silk tunic, over which she wore a white kaftan with embroidered cartridge pouches on the chest, on which fell the ropes of Portland pearls. On her head was a tall Astrakhan fez."

The Bloomsbury crowd – notably the Stephen sisters, Virginia and Vanessa, Lytton Strachey, and Roger Fry – ensured the bohemian bona fides of "Our Lady of Bedford Square." Hungry artists could always be certain of a decent spread and a handout. The painter Augustus John assured her that she did not need to prove her generosity to him, but that was after she had already slept with him. Artists Jacob Epstein and Henry Lamb were not so proud and accepted her financial assistance and adulation as their due. Henry James, who despised these "irreverent young people," stood with her one evening on the landing looking down at the boisterous crowd below. "Look at them," he warned her. "Look at them, dear lady, over the banisters. But don't go down amongst them." It was a warning she chose to ignore and would later have good cause to recall.

Although her salon was flourishing, Ottoline was not yet satisfied, and her status as London's paramount hostess had failed to sate a gnawing emotional hunger. Her torrid affair with Bertrand Russell, begun in 1911, seemed to hold great promise, but Russell, who exploited their relationship to disentangle himself from a loveless marriage, would never regard her as an equal. "He told me that I could never accomplish anything important in life by *my reading* while I could help by being with him," she wrote in her *Memoirs*. "The great thing seems to me in dealing with people is to find the *centre* of a human being, their core, to get into touch with that, and from that to radiate out in understanding." This foolhardy quest was never going to be realized in a busy, transient, fashion-conscious London salon. Through the glory years of Edwardian indulgence, she gradually came to the conviction that what she really wanted was to "collect people . . . and make a more complete compact society of intellectuals." Only in such a setting could she indulge her "one touch of genius . . . the power of loving people."

In 1915, she got her chance. Ostensibly out of concern for Julian's delicate health, the Morrells left London for the Jacobean manor of Garsington, in Oxfordshire. In her memoirs, Ottoline limned her aspirations: "I should like to make this place into a harbour, a refuge in the storm, where those who haven't been swept away could come and renew themselves and go forth strengthened." With hindsight, she added. "But people are very difficult to manage." It was to be a retreat and an egalitarian utopia, with Ottoline in the role of angel presiding over a community of brilliant, liberated, and grateful artists and writers. She painted one drawing room Venetian red to match her hair, the entrance hall dove gray, and the sitting room peacock green, with gold moldings. She filled the house with oriental boxes, cabinets, china, and hangings. The scent of incense, potpourri, and clove-studded oranges permeated the manor. She converted an old fish pond into a swimming pool with an ornamental island at the center. As Virginia Woolf said of the place, "I think even the sky is done up in pale yellow silk, and certainly the cabbages are scented."

When she was thoroughly satisfied that all had been done to make the artists feel relaxed and at home, Ottoline opened the doors to her eager guests. "This ornate, other-worldly environment was soon the Mecca of all aspiring young writers and artists," writes Michael Holroyd. "From being a highly fashionable meeting-place, Garsington was quickly transformed into a cultural legend."

Almost from the outset, Garsington proved to be a naïve proposal ripe with portents of disaster. The artists and writers showed up in droves – D. H. Lawrence, Aldous Huxley, Roger Fry, Dora Carrington, Clive Bell, Lytton Strachey, Katherine Mansfield, Virginia Woolf, and Robert Graves, among others –

immediately ensuring that Garsington would be "a bedlam of conflicting egotisms." Some came for the weekend; others for the year. The painter Dorothy Brett stayed three years. They ate Ottoline's food and complained about it. She provided towels and bathing suits; after a swim, the guests would "sit or lie on the lawn endlessly talking, talking." Many who sought to evade military service were provided the legal alternative of agricultural labor on the working farm, although few did any farming. As dedicated pacifists, Ottoline and Philip declined to promote the war effort, but they did invite many of the wounded to recuperate at Garsington. The Morrells, who never enjoyed great wealth, were perennially strapped, but the guests kept coming. And staying. And backbiting.

However clueless Ottoline may have been about artists' capacity for gratitude, she was not unaware that many took her hospitality for granted. Siegfried Sassoon may have been briefly right that, although already into her forties, she had yet to learn that "the writers and artists whom she befriended were capable of proving ungrateful," but she was learning fast. Only a year after opening Garsington, she was referring in her journal to "This crowd of crude and selfish people which have invaded us." She elaborated on this theme in her memoirs:

Sometimes I used to feel hurt when people came and did not trouble to talk to me, but just amused themselves and ignored me. When I was talking to Gilbert Cannan one day I said that I felt that the young people who came looked on me as a sort of kind manageress of a hotel, and he rather took me aback by saying, "Of course, we do."

Others noticed, too. Referring to "the horror of the Garsington situation," Virginia Woolf wrote that "O. and P. and the house provide a good deal, which isn't accepted very graciously." Ottoline tried to take it in her stride, noting that "I can go my own way and let them go theirs," yet conveniently forgetting that she was already going her own way. But she could not entirely repress a dawning awareness of the reality that was evident to everyone around her. "It is exhausting to give and give . . . without any return. One deludes oneself with the belief that by giving one will receive something, but it isn't true."

What she was probably unaware of, at least at first, was the extent to which they not only took advantage of her, but also mocked her behind her back. Even the compliments of good friends had a nasty edge to them. "Lady Ottoline was the only person I have ever seen who could look, at one and the same moment, beautiful and what I can only call grotesque," wrote Lord David Cecil. "The house is . . . very like Ottoline herself, in fact – very remarkable, very impressive, patched, gilded and preposterous," noted Lytton Strachey. They coined cruel nicknames for her, such as "the Old Ott" and "Lady Omega Muddle." Dora Carrington seems to have been among the few guests to sympathize. "What traitors all these people are! They ridicule Ottoline! . . . I think it's beastly of them to enjoy Ottoline's kindness and then laugh at her."

The financial and emotional investments in Garsington had been substantial, however, and Ottoline stoically continued to endure their diminishing returns. How long this state of affairs might have lasted is anyone's guess, but sooner or later something had to give, and in 1917 that something was D. H. Lawrence, who had been one of Garsington's very first and most pampered guests. *Women in Love* was not the first time Ottoline had been portrayed as a fictional character – she had been somewhat crudely fictionalized by a lovesick professor, John Adam Cramb (writing as J. A. Revermort), in his 1910 novel

Cuthbert Learmont. But Lawrence's Hermione Roddice, a member of "the slack aristocracy that keeps touch with the arts," was of a different order:

> She was impressive . . . yet macabre, something repulsive. People were silent when she passed, impressed, roused, wanting to jeer, yet for some reason silenced. Her long, pale face, that she carried lifted up, somewhat in the Rossetti fashion, seemed almost drugged, as if a strange mass of thoughts coiled in the darkness within her, and she was never allowed to escape.

The portrait of Hermione may also have been particularly painful to Ottoline for being so close to the mark:

> She suffered a torture, under her confidence and her pride, feeling herself exposed to wounds and to mockery and to despite. She always felt vulnerable, vulnerable, there was always a secret chink in her armour. She did not know herself what it was. It was a lack of robust self, she had no natural sufficiency, there was a terrible void, a lack, a deficiency of being within her."

All of her friends had read Lawrence's manuscript. Ottoline recognized herself in Hermione and took it as a personal betrayal. "Chapter after chapter, scene after scene, all written, as far as I could tell, in order to humiliate me . . . I showed it to Aldous . . . and he was equally horrified." Lawrence, it goes without saying, was banished.

But *Women in Love* was just 1917's opening salvo. That year, long-suffering Philip finally went ahead and found himself a lover. Worse yet, Bertrand Russell initiated a yearlong affair with

Lady Constance Malleson, claiming that Ottoline was very "un-instinctive and . . . entirely lacking in the qualities that would make me a comfortable companion." Then, she found herself snubbed by Katherine Mansfield when Mansfield's husband, critic John Middleton Murry, claimed that she had made advances toward him. A nasty case of the measles capped a very bad year for Ottoline.

A diary entry for November sums up her heartbreak and disillusion:

> It is like death, though still alive, the death of all illusions, death of desire. Everyone that I thought was a friend has shrivelled up, faded away. It is not their fault, only the result of their characters. But now I see them clearly as they are, without the veil of illusion that I had clothed them in, and I see that what one individual can give to another is infinitely small. I dreamt that I could give my friends something wonderful, but now I see that to them it isn't wonderful . . . most people live in a steaming cauldron of resentments, irritation and dislike and envy and have only a varnish of decent behaviour.

The year 1918 brought fleeting relief. "This is too beautiful, it cannot last," she wrote on getting rid of the last of her guests. She was right. The ensuing years would see no fewer than three new fictional portraits, two of them by her beloved friend Aldous Huxley, the betrayal made all the worse by the fact that he had witnessed the pain caused by *Women in Love*. In Huxley's first novel, 1921's *Crome Yellow*, she is Priscilla Wimbush; in his second, 1925's *Those Barren Leaves*, she is Lilian Aldwinkle. In both cases, it was not only she but also all of Garsington that were satirized. "How could he, who had lived with us in such intimacy, so violate the human decencies as to mock and ridicule the life in which, after all, he had partaken with such apparent pleasure and happiness?" How indeed?

Life at Garsington did not come to an end after the war, but the old spirit of recklessness and mayhem was gone. In the place of the bohemians came a more staid crowd: Ezra Pound, T. S. Eliot, Siegfried Sassoon, the latter so embarrassed to be seen with her in public that he hid until he could be sure she was dressed with restraint. But the Jazz Age was coming, and younger, wealthier hostesses, such as Nancy Cunard and Lady Colefax, were siphoning off her guests back in London. By 1927, when the novelist W. J. Turner parodied her one last time in his book *The Aesthetes*, it hardly seemed to matter anymore, or to hurt. Turner likens his heroine, Lady Virginia Caraway, to Switzerland, the Russian Ballet, and the Tower of Pisa: "She is known only to tourists or sight-seers. They look at her and go away – and write books about her." That year, broke and dispirited, Ottoline and Philip sold Garsington and retreated to London.

Like Ottoline Morrell, Gertrude Stein (1874–1946) was the youngest of five siblings. Unlike Ottoline, Gertrude believed in her own genius. Indeed, she believed that there were only three living geniuses in the world: Pablo Picasso, Alfred North Whitehead (coauthor with Bertrand Russell of the *Principia Mathematica*), and herself. She believed, according to one source, that "nobody has done anything to develop the English language since Shakespeare, except myself, and Henry James perhaps a little." She believed that "the Jews have produced only three originative geniuses: Christ, Spinoza, and myself." Of the latter in particular she was firmly convinced; her life's work was to convince the world of it, which she ultimately did – at least to her own satisfaction.

But all of that was many years off when she joined her brother

Leo in Paris in 1903, where he was trying to learn to paint and had rented himself a studio and home at 27, rue de Fleurus, on the Left Bank. Stein had been raised in some affluence in California, studied at Radcliffe under William James, and spent several years at Johns Hopkins School of Medicine before flunking out from sheer boredom. Now, at twenty-nine, with a couple of rehearsal manuscripts lying in a drawer somewhere, she was going to launch a new life as a writer. Believing as she did that the United States, having launched the modern era, was the oldest country in the world, simply being a writer was not going to be enough. She was to be the *first* writer of the modern age and her book *Three Lives* the first work of literary modernism. But there were a few distractions on the way.

Leo, like many progressive gentlemen of his day, was an avid collector of Japanese prints in 1903. But he had recently gotten wind of a little-known painter, an old man whose unusual works were said to be considerably cheaper than Japanese prints. After a visit to the gallery of Ambroise Vollard, the only dealer in Paris to sell this painter's work, Leo and Gertrude walked out with a luminous landscape, their first Cézanne. The following year, a small windfall of about sixteen hundred dollars from their father's estate allowed them to pick up two more Cézannes, a couple of Gauguins, and some Renoirs. Leo and Gertrude started dressing in cheap brown corduroy and sandals to save money to buy art. Their economies netted them works by Degas, Delacroix, Manet, and Toulouse-Lautrec.

In 1905, they attended the Autumn Salon to consider the work of nonestablishment painters. The scandal of *La femme au chapeau* – a rough portrait of garish colors that was eliciting howls of outrage throughout the capital and had provoked one journalist into slanging the artist as a wild beast, or *fauve* – had attracted their attention. The painter was asking five hundred francs (about one hundred dollars); the Steins offered four hundred, the painter held out for his asking price, and the Steins caved. In this way, the Steins became the principal patrons of Henri Matisse, who, at the time of the Salon, was being supported by the income from his wife's millinery shop.

The Steins continued to acquire Matisses over the next few years, becoming good friends of the artist and his wife. Gradually, the Japanese prints came down. Soon, there was no room left on the apartment walls and Leo started hanging his pictures in the painting studio. Word spread of the unorthodox collection, which the Steins generously opened to anyone who cared to view it. "Matisse brought people, everybody brought somebody, and they came at any time and it began to be a nuisance, and it was in this way that Saturday evenings began." 27, rue de Fleurus was on its way to becoming what James R. Mellow would call "a ministry of propaganda for modern art."

From the very beginning, the Steins' Saturday "at homes" were essentially open houses. All you needed was an introduction to attend. *"De la part de qui venez-vous?"* Gertrude would ask at the door. "By whose invitation are you here?" On at least one occasion, the new arrival was there by her own invitation, which she had extended and promptly forgotten. He would be ushered through the interior courtyard into the crowded studio, where Leo harangued the throng with passionate and learned discourses on the new art. The paintings rose in tiers to the ceiling, the higher ones all but invisible in the dim gas light. Gertrude sat silent and Buddha-like, her legs tucked under her ample frame, on an overstuffed armchair to the side. It was a position she was to maintain with increasing comfort for the next thirty years.

Special friends – the Matisses, the Picassos, Georges Braque, André Derain, Marie Laurencin, Marcel Duchamp, Marsden Hartley, Charles Demuth, Arthur Dove, a very young Joseph

Stella, and the poets Guillaume Apollinaire and Max Jacob among them – were invited to supper before the salon, where they were served simple meals, roasts and omelettes. Matisse once offended the Steins' cook, Hélène, by asking about the evening's menu before accepting an invitation. Hélène considered such rudeness acceptable in a foreigner but not in a Frenchman, and thereafter served fried eggs instead of omelettes whenever he attended. After the meal, the artists were served up to the hungry crowd in the studio. James Mellow writes:

> Inevitably, the tourists came because it was the thing to do when one was in Paris. A few went away converted, spreading the gospel of modernism among the heathen, sending fresh troops for later visits. Others came to scoff at the pictures, barely able to conceal their laughter before the doors closed behind them. Some came purposely to bait the artists.

The Steins bought their first Picasso, *La jeune fille aux fleurs*, in 1905. Gertrude hated the painting but grudgingly allowed Leo to acquire it. When they sought out the young artist in his studio, however, she was immediately drawn to him and they struck up a friendship that was to endure for the next forty years. They spent $150 on that first visit and came away with "scores" of paintings from his blue and rose periods. The following year, after great struggle, he produced his *Portrait of Gertrude Stein*, an important transitional work on the way to cubism, which emerged full-blown in 1907 with *Les Demoiselles d'Avignon*. Although he had been Picasso's initial champion, Leo reviled the new development, whereas Gertrude reveled in it. From that moment, Picasso and Gertrude owned the modernist movement, and Matisse and Leo found themselves on the sidelines. Gertrude usurped Leo's role as oracle, and young men began to gather at her feet to look and listen in veneration. It was at this juncture that she began to assume the appurtenances of "a Sumerian monument."

It was also in 1907 (just as Ottoline Morrell was inaugurating her Thursday evenings on Bedford Square) that Gertrude first met Alice Babette Toklas, who was to become her lifelong companion and factotum, further accelerating Gertrude's alienation from her brother. Although they had been each other's vital companions in earlier years, after Leo eventually moved to Italy in 1913 they never spoke again.

At this point, Gertrude Stein had had little success with her own writing, nor would she for many years afterward. It is true that many an intelligent critic has dismissed her talents as obscure or illusory. Her own brother (admittedly embittered) once told a friend that "you have no idea how dumb she is" and that "Gertrude can't think consecutively for ten seconds," but that is beside the point. Much of her work may be impenetrable and numbingly repetitive, but there is no doubt that no one was writing like her at the time, and since she was at least partially responsible for discovering the work of the century's best artists when they had few other boosters, she may perhaps be forgiven for assuming her intuition to be infallible when it came to her own genius. Boastful she certainly was – intolerably so to those in whom she had no interest – but her arrogance was of far greater benefit to her artists than it ever proved to herself.

She eventually managed to publish *Three Lives* in 1909 at her own expense (six hundred dollars), selling fewer than a hundred copies in the first eighteen months but garnering some favorable reviews. It also brought her work to the attention of a generation of American writers that would rise to prominence with her name balanced reverentially on the tips of their tongues, like a communion wafer. Roger Fry's writing about Stein in the *Burlington Review* prompted visits by Augustus John, Henry Lamb, and their patron. "There was Lady Ottoline Morrell looking like a marvelous feminine version of Disraeli and tall and strange shyly hesitating at the door," Stein would later write. Stein's reciprocating visit to Garsington a few years later was not a success, as she was unable to abide the "continuous pleasant hesitating flow of conversation, the never ceasing sound of the human voice speaking in english."

The truth is, Stein would essentially remain a figure of ridicule and bemusement to the general public until the astounding commercial success of *The Autobiography of Alice B. Toklas* in 1933. She was the high priestess of a dangerous and arcane cult, revered by her followers, feared and maligned by the rest. Although often bitter about her lack of publishing success, especially as so many younger writers in her stable rose to fame, she was self-confident enough to amortize her image as a "pagan idol" and to scorn popular opinion. The 1913 Armory Show in New York, to which she loaned many of the most important works, only heightened that reputation, but it was the 1914 publication of *Tender Buttons* that sealed it, spawning a raft of malicious parodies of her style. *Tender Buttons*, she claimed, "had an enormous influence on all young writers and started off columnists in the newspapers of the whole country on their long campaign of ridicule." She would read the best of these out loud to Alice and chuckle.

The outbreak of war caught her in England, visiting with Alfred North Whitehead. She and Alice spent much of the following two years in Spain, but eventually she was overcome by a strong need to involve herself in the war effort and returned to France in 1916. She had a Ford truck shipped from the United States and fitted out as an ambulance, which she drove for the American Fund for French Wounded. Throughout the rest of the war, working in Perpignan and Nîmes, she delivered medical supplies and adopted numerous military "god-sons," to whom she wrote long letters after their return to the front. For her efforts, she was ultimately awarded the Médaille de la Reconnaissance Française.

After the war and some civilian relief work in Alsace, she and Alice returned to the rue de Fleurus but did not resume their Saturday evenings. Too much had changed. It was "very difficult to think back and remember what happened before." Apollinaire was dead; she and Picasso were (temporarily) on the outs; Matisse was in Nice; Juan Gris was sick. "We saw a tremendous number of people but none of them as far as I can remember that we had ever known before."

Still, Stein remained the patron saint of the avant-garde and continued to take her role seriously, befriending the young American writers and artists who flocked to Paris in the Jazz Age. By 1926, Janet Flanner was able to write in *The New Yorker*: "No American writer is taken more seriously than Miss Stein by the Paris modernists." Those who sought her out, called her friend, and enjoyed her hospitality included Sherwood Anderson, Ernest Hemingway, Djuna Barnes, Virgil Thomson, Paul Bowles, and Glenway Wescott, but they did not come for her help and patronage – they came for her benediction.

It is not difficult to come up with any number of reasons why Ottoline Morrell ultimately failed and Gertrude Stein succeeded as patrons and hostesses. Stein had an abundance of self-confidence and hubris where Ottoline had none. Stein's primary identity was as a creator and artist in her own right and she was able to look even the most arrogant of her benefactees in the eye. Ottoline had little "natural sufficiency" and her artists could not help but recognize and disdain the vicarious nature of her attachment to them. Both had plenty of vocal detractors, but in Stein the waves of ridicule ran up against an impervious dike, while they simply overwhelmed and swept away Morrell's castle of sand. Many of Ottoline's guests, including Virginia Woolf and D. H. Lawrence, mistrusted and resented what they saw as her aristocratic maternalism, whereas Stein's salon was always and emphatically democratic and inclusive. Then, too, it was a question of their respective guest lists: Stein's Frenchmen, Spaniards, and Americans were thirsty and excitable, whereas Ottoline's Englishmen were jaded by class distinctions and bitter, especially during and after the war.

All of these are reasonable and acceptable explanations, but they do not necessarily provide us with insight into the true nature of our hospitality and the secret currency of human transactions. After all, each of us knows people endowed with extraordinary arrogance or insuperable insecurities – often both together. Many may be extremely and generously hospitable, but few are so rash as to open their home and wallet (let alone the fortress of their ego) to hungry, self-centered, and ungrateful artists. And with good reason: you may be able to persuade a group of stock analysts to line up obediently before a bowl of iced Beluga and a bottle of '71 Chateau Pétrus, but artists are harder to wrangle. They do not necessarily respond to the standard stimuli of hospitality. Any host determined to transform her guests into teddy bears had better stalk tamer game unless she is very sure of herself, because this exercise is certain to strip away the comforting illusions about hospitality, revealing the ugly bedrock truth that we would all prefer to remain buried: no one, wealthy arts patrons least of all, gives something for nothing. Even when she is not sure of what she is after, even when she is unconscious of having an agenda, a host expects a return on her largesse. It may be and is likely to be an intangible return, banked only in hidden vaults, but it must be made if the contract between host and guest is to prove profitable to both.

The guest senses this even more acutely than the host – who may be blinded by a dazzling perception of her own disinterest – and is constantly seeking clues and signals as to the nature of the host's desires. It is only when the host is somehow able to communicate those desires – when she has exercised her will upon her teddy bears – that the experience of her hospitality will be positive and fruitful for both. When her signals are murky and half-hearted, when she speaks her strength but acts her weakness, when she seeks more than she can or is willing to give, the guest has every right to feel cheated and to turn against his would-be partner.

Gertrude Stein understood this. She offered leadership for solidarity, and it was a fair deal for everyone. Ottoline Morrell did not. She offered tea and cakes in return for a natural sufficiency that no one could give her. It was a preposterous proposal, and they all laughed at her. If you pretend to feed a teddy bear, he will pretend to eat, and you will both be happy. If you try to force-feed him, you will both end up covered in slop.

CHAPTER III

ODD FISH

The host in the role of confidence man never inspires faith.
Richard Ellsworth Call, *The Life and Writings of Rafinesque*

In the spring of 1818, a weary traveler disembarked from a small boat on the Ohio River at the village of Henderson, Kentucky. Carrying what appeared to be a sheaf of dried clover on his back, wearing a badly stained and worn suit of yellow nankeen and pantaloons buttoned down to the ankles, and sporting a long beard and lank black hair below his shoulders, the traveler gave every appearance of being a wandering quack or herbalist of no social standing. Approaching the first person he met on the riverbank, he asked in a heavy French accent for directions to the grocer's house. The man happened to be that very grocer and told him so. The traveler then presented the grocer with a letter of introduction from a mutual acquaintance in Lexington.

"I send you an odd fish," the brief letter read, "which you may prove to be undescribed." The grocer asked the traveler if he might see the fish. The traveler smiled with good humor.

"I am that odd fish I presume," he said.

In Greek, the word for hospitality is *xenia*, derived from *xenos*, meaning "stranger" or "foreigner." Although *xenia* was a central element of Greek culture, the word survives in common English only as the root of *xenophobia*, with very negative connotations. Our word *hospitality*, on the other hand, comes from the Latin *hospes*, meaning "host," as well as "guest," and which itself is a condensed form of *hostipotis*, meaning "lord of strangers." In other words, the Greek concept of hospitality was based on the primacy of the guest, whereas the Latin concept, which we inherited, was based on that of the host. In ancient Greece, the host always sat in the smaller chair, lower than that of the guest; with us, the host sits at the head of the table. In Greece, even the wealthiest host served simple dishes designed solely to satisfy a guest's hunger; with the Romans, as with us, elaborate culinary constructs serve mostly to highlight the host's tastes and skills. Some may argue that our espousal of the Latin model has nothing to do with cultural identity, but that is clearly not so. We choose our words to fit our ideas, and the Latin fit better than the Greek. In the West, it is the role of the host that matters, for he is lord of strangers.

I must admit, to my chagrin, that almost everyone who gets to enjoy my hospitality is a friend, or at least someone I know. I wish I could say that, like the Greeks, we make friends and connections by offering food and shelter to strangers, but that doesn't seem to be the way in New York City. We make friends by going to someone else's house and meeting their friends, which is not terrible per se, but may be limiting. You tend to meet more people like yourself that way, people who probably don't need more friends and who are almost certainly not strangers stranded in a foreign city, for whom hospitality is more than just a pleasant way to while away an evening.

As an example of just how limiting this approach can be, my wife and I recently learned of a dinner party given by friends of ours, to which we had not been invited. That was fine, of course, but we were dismayed to discover that they had invited friends of ours whom they had met at a dinner we had given several weeks earlier. Everyone we spoke to agreed that it was at the very least bad manners to exclude us, the introducers, from their first unmediated encounter. There was a sense of poaching in the reproach, almost as if something had been stolen from us. At the time, I shared the general feeling that a wrong had been committed, but I've changed my mind. A host, I've come to see, should aspire to be the lord of strangers, not the lord of friends of friends.

Many anthropologists believe that hospitality arose as an adjunct to long-distance trade. Long before *xenia* even, Mesopotamian traveling merchants were compelled to rely on strangers for shelter in a world without hotels. Brillat-Savarin claimed that hospitality began as protection for travelers who brought news from other lands, a sort of primordial diplomatic immunity. However it may have begun, reliance on strangers for hospitality was ubiquitous in ancient and medieval Europe.

It was also a prominent feature of life on the American frontier – such as Henderson, Kentucky, in 1818 – where white settlements were few and far between, inns and other amenities scarce, and currency either unavailable or unreliable as a means of exchange. You had little choice: if you were planning to travel west, beyond the States, you had better line up your letters of introduction well in advance, because you were going to be sleeping in the homes of strangers. You would need to feel comfortable that you could trust them, as they would you.

The traveler in yellow and the grocer had much in common, though they didn't know it. Both were native French speakers, the sons of successful merchants, who had fled to the United States in their youth to escape being drafted into Napoleon's armies. Both had arrived in calamitous circumstances – the traveler in a near fatal shipwreck, the grocer with a near fatal case of yellow fever. Neither had a formal higher education. Both had spent arduous years of wilderness trekking throughout the vast country. Both were ambitious and driven men, yet neither was able to make any sort of a living at his chosen calling. Both were considered to be exceedingly unconventional by those who knew them, and both were naturalists. The grocer was John James Audubon, who twenty years later was to be the most celebrated artist and ornithologist in the New World. The traveler was Constantine Samuel Rafinesque-Schmaltz, a prolific autodidact with a modest but growing reputation as a discoverer of new species, who twenty-two years later would die alone, penniless, and unmourned in a garret on Race Street in Philadelphia. Their encounter in Henderson was, in some measure, to contribute to the fates of both.

Whatever Audubon and Rafinesque had in common was essentially superficial, but their differences were critical. Whereas Audubon was consistently characterized as "simple" (in the sense of unaffected), Rafinesque could never shake "eccentric." Audubon was charming, handsome, and well-groomed, a born storyteller and talented musician at a time when and in a place where home entertainment was pretty much the only entertainment. Although the next few years were to prove extremely difficult for him following a painful bankruptcy, he was always able to get what he needed out of people, especially women. He had a devoted and doting family willing to put up with years of absence and penury for the sake of his professional advancement.

Rafinesque, on the other hand, was perennially unkempt, physically unimposing, socially awkward, absentminded, and the object of some ridicule and contempt among his peers. In the 1890s, Richard Ellsworth Call interviewed several people who had known him in their youth: "Careless of his style of dressing, indeed, his clothes never fitted him and appeared to have been made for some one else . . . an eccentric man"; "a man of peculiar habits and . . . very eccentric"; "He was a stranger . . . all the young people made jokes at his expense . . . he knew none of the arts that make a man popular"; "A small, peculiar looking Italian . . . very scientific, absorbed in his books and his bugs, his researches and his writings . . . an innocent, inoffensive sort of man."

Naturalism in the United States was then in its infancy and anyone who wanted to make a name for himself in the field had to be ready to head into the wilderness to seek new species. He also had to be able to record what he had seen, in drawing and in accurate, scientifically grounded notes. Audubon was a keen outdoorsman, a superb shot, and a robust camper, able to endure enormous hardship for the sake of capturing one new finch on paper. He was, of course, a brilliant artist and a tireless observer. Rafinesque – although gifted with occasionally brilliant insight and credited by some with having discovered "the basic law of change in species some twenty years or more before Charles Darwin" – was a terrible draftsman and an unreliable note-taker who went into the field in the summer but waited until winter to draft his observations. He was an impatient researcher and a foolishly rash publisher who "once sent for publication a paper describing, in regular natural history style, twelve new species of thunder and lightning which he had observed near the Falls of the Ohio." As David Starr Jordan, first president of Stanford University, noted, "Rafinesque's work as a whole is bad enough, and bad in a peculiarly original and exasperating way." Another refers to "the beauty of the quaint French penmanship and the atrocious badness of the accompanying drawings." Although he crossed the Alleghenies five times on foot, once registering twelve hundred miles in a single year, he was out of place in nature, where he was tormented by weather, hunger, and biting insects and where, by his own admission, he carried an umbrella.

Of all the differences between the two men, perhaps the most telling was Audubon's ferocious single-mindedness. From his earliest days, he had had one ambition and one ambition only: to draw and be recognized as the world's foremost artist of nature. From early adulthood, his entire life and substance were devoted to that purpose. He left his beloved sons and wife for years on end to raise money and support for his project and, when in the field, often spent eighteen hours a day shooting, drawing, and taking notes. Rafinesque was, to put it mildly, eclectic. Although he always considered himself to be a naturalist, he also boasted without irony of having been a botanist, geologist, geographer, historian, poet, philosopher, philologist, economist, philanthropist, traveler, merchant, manufacturer, brewer, collector, improver, teacher, surveyor, draughtsman, architect, engineer, palmist, author, editor, bookseller, librarian, and secretary. "I hardly know what I may not become as yet, since, whenever I apply myself to anything which I like, I never fail to succeed," he wrote with considerable exaggeration.

Up to the moment of their encounter, Rafinesque had endured the same sort of ill fortune that would continue to pursue him throughout his remaining days. Born in Galata, near Constantinople, in 1783, he was raised in Marseilles and Genoa. He lost his father to yellow fever when he was ten and his father's fortune to a dishonest partner. His mother, a timorous German, kept him locked away from the rest of the world, educated him with private tutors, and generally left him "largely unprepared to defend himself in an aggressive, selfish world." It did not help that his sole passion was botany, a solitary vocation. With Napoleon's recruiters closing in, she shipped him off to Philadelphia in 1802, where he toiled as a shipping clerk while scouring the countryside for specimens.

He returned to Italy in 1804, moving to Sicily where he lived for the next ten years. He worked as secretary to the United States consul and as the manager of a whiskey distillery before making a small fortune exporting medicinal squill, a wild herb which he allowed the Sicilians to believe was being used in the manufacture of dye. He married and had two children, a daughter and a son who died in infancy. When the Sicilians came to understand how profitable his business was and cut off their dealings with him, and when his wife took up with a squalid comedian named Giovanni Pizzarrone, he decided to cash in his chips and head back to the States. For Rafinesque, Sicily had become a land of "fruitful soil, delightful climate, excellent productions, perfidious men, deceitful women."

On November 2, 1815, his ship lost its keel off Race Rocks, at the eastern end of Long Island. "I had lost every thing, my fortune, my share of the cargo, my collections and labors for 20 years past, my books, my manuscripts, my drawings, even my clothes . . . I walked to New London." He eventually found his way to New York, where he worked for a time as private tutor to the Livingston family in Clermont. But it was the opening West, with its uncounted new species of plants and fish, that held his fascination. Traveling almost exclusively by foot through New York state, New Jersey, Delaware, and Pennsylvania, he gradually made his way to Kentucky, where an old family friend recommended him for a job as professor of natural history and modern languages at Transylvania University, in Lexington. It was to this, the sole of the many academic posts to which he applied that he was ever appointed to, that he was headed when he stopped off in Henderson. If anyone in the world needed a helping hand and a sympathetic ear in the wilderness, it was Rafinesque.

He was warmly welcomed into the modest but respectable Audubon log cabin, which was only too well accustomed to accommodating travelers and itinerant family members. He amused the occupants by refusing to change his filthy clothes and by his very apparent reluctance to wash before dinner. Upon examining Audubon's drawings, he categorically refused to believe that one plant depicted therein really existed until Audubon led him to the riverbank to observe the original. When convinced, he danced with joy, hugged Audubon, and there and then declared the discovery of a new genus. Still, despite the visitor's eccentricities, Audubon claims to have found him charming and erudite. "I listened to him with as much delight as Telemachus could have listened to Mentor."

Late on the night of Rafinesque's arrival, when all but Audubon were asleep, the household was disturbed by an almighty racket coming from the naturalist's room. Audubon rushed to the scene of the commotion:

I saw my guest running about the room naked, holding the handle of my favorite violin, the body of which he had battered to pieces against the walls in attempting to kill the bats which had entered by the open window, probably attracted by the insects flying around his candle. I stood amazed, but he continued jumping and running round and round, until he was fairly exhausted, when he begged me to procure one of the animals for him, as he felt convinced they belonged to "a new species." Although I was convinced of the contrary, I took up the bow of my demolished Cremona, and administering a smart tap to each of the bats as it came up, soon got specimens enough. The war ended, I again bade him good night, but could not help observing the state of the room. It was strewed with plants, which it would seem he had arranged into groups, but which were now scattered about in confusion. "Never mind, Mr AUDUBON," quoth the eccentric naturalist, "never mind, I'll soon arrange them again. I have the bats, and that's enough."

Over the next few days, the men went their separate ways, Audubon attending to his store and birds, Rafinesque searching the woods for plants. When Rafinesque expressed his desire to see an authentic canebrake, Audubon was unable to resist the opportunity to avenge his destroyed Cremona. He had clearly sized up his guest as an inadequate woodsman, wholly unsuited to exploring dense and dangerous canebrakes, "the usual mode of passing through [which] is by pushing one's self backward, and wedging a way between the stems." He led Rafinesque to the densest canebrake in the vicinity. When Rafinesque fled and collapsed in terror at the appearance of a bear, Audubon could not help but laugh out loud at his "ridiculous exhibition." He also lied outright to the exhausted Rafinesque by assuring him that their worst difficulties were nearly over, knowing full well that they still had miles to go. "I kept my companion in such constant difficulties, that he now panted, perspired, and seemed almost overcome by fatigue . . . I kept him tumbling and crawling on his hands and knees." Audubon secretly exulted when they were drenched in a downpour; Rafinesque had apparently left his umbrella in Henderson. In an effort to lighten his load, the naturalist abandoned all of the valuable plant specimens he had collected along the way. They eventually emerged onto the riverbank and were ferried back to town.

Rafinesque remained with the Audubons for a full three weeks, "but never again expressed a desire of visiting a cane-brake." Then one night he disappeared. He was sought high and low, to no avail, and the Audubons feared the worst. His evaporation remained a mystery for several weeks until the Audubons received a thank-you note from him, presumably sent from Lexington.

Some thirteen years after the encounter, Audubon included a six-page account of this visit in the first volume of his *Ornithological Biography*, the textual accompaniment to his *Birds of America*. By the time of its publication, Audubon was well established on the path that was to lead to international fame, while Rafinesque was already deep into his professional decline, having been hounded in the most humiliating fashion from his post at Transylvania University in 1826. "The Eccentric Naturalist" is written in such a way as to shed the utmost possible ridicule on its subject, quite cruelly in view of the broad professional readership that Audubon could anticipate. Although he disguises Rafinesque under the pseudonym "M. de T.," no one was fooled. Everyone was able to recognize, in the words of one anonymous observer, the "genius with many peculiarities and not much dignity." Oddly enough, Rafinesque praised "The Eccentric Naturalist" when it was published, calling Audubon "my friend," but by that time he was probably grateful for recognition of any sort.

If so, he was almost certainly unaware of the even greater injustice Audubon, in his role as trusted host and intellectual peer, had inflicted on him thirteen years earlier. Audubon makes no mention of the prank in "The Eccentric Naturalist" and seems, presumably for shame, to have shared it with very few. It only came to light some fifty-five years later, retailed by David Starr Jordan in a paper read before the Indiana Academy of Sciences on December 30, 1885, and subsequently published in *The Popular Science Monthly*. Jordan had received the story from one Dr. Kirtland, who had heard it directly from John Bachman, Audubon's great friend whose daughters were married to Audubon's sons.

When Audubon claims in "The Eccentric Naturalist" that "M. de T. although a highly scientific man, was suspicious to a fault, and believed such plants only to exist as he had himself seen," he was being entirely disingenuous. In fact, he was concealing the trail of a miserable fraud that he himself had perpetrated. It seems that, during the course of Rafinesque's stay in Henderson, Audubon had given him some ten drawings of fantastic and imaginary fish that he claimed to have personally observed in the Ohio. Although these creatures are entirely implausible, Rafinesque – ever in thrall to his impatience, excitability, and childlike enthusiasms – fell for them hook, line, and sinker, as Audubon must have known he would.

Even if it had gone no further, it would have been a cruel enough trick to play on anyone who was such an easy mark and so far out of his element. But it did go further. Rafinesque subsequently named and published these findings in his *Ichthyologia Ohiensis*, declaring the discovery of such new genera as *Pogostoma, Aplocentrus, Litholepis*, and *Pilodictis*. One fish, the "devil-jack diamond-fish" (*Litholepis adamantinus*), supposedly grew up to ten feet long and weighed four hundred pounds. Sleeping on the surface of the water and often mistaken for a log, it had "scales as hard as flint, and even proof against lead balls! . . . they strike fire with steel!" It seems incredible that Rafinesque would publish such findings without proof, until we remember that all of his information had been "communicated to me by Mr. Audubon," a man whom he respected and had no reason to mistrust. (This incriminating evidence went unnoticed because it was published long before Audubon achieved fame.) After all, as far as Rafinesque was concerned, Audubon had been an exemplary host and generous guide in the wilderness.

Because the prank went undiscovered during Rafinesque's

lifetime, it did immeasurable harm to his reputation. The *Ichthyologia Ohiensis* continued to be a puzzle and a torment to ichthyologists for many years, since no one but Rafinesque ever succeeded in identifying the mythological creatures it describes. It led to the general opinion among his peers that "he had described certainly twice as many fishes, and probably nearly twice as many plants and shells, also, as really existed in the regions over which he traveled." His few remaining supporters began to melt away. Already widely disliked and dismissed by his colleagues for his rash denunciations and his monomania on the subject of new species, as well as for his lack of scientific rigor, Rafinesque had been hanging on to respectability by a thread. His *Ichthyologia* cut it. Even today, more than 160 years after his death, his work continues to be debunked. One noted scholar, David Oestreicher, recently disproved Rafinesque's claim to have discovered the *Walum Olum*, an epic saga written in pictographs on tree bark, supposedly documenting the Lenape tribe's migration to North America from Siberia across the frozen Bering Strait.

His declining years in Philadelphia tell a miserable tale of desperation, paranoia, and grandiosity. He became the kind of man who refers to his perceived enemies as "the foes of mankind." While writing, seemingly, on every subject under the sun – from the principles of wealth and safe banking, through the Hebrew Bible, to the cure for consumption, not to mention a two-hundred-page poem titled *The World; Or, Instability* – he claimed to have invented coupon bonds, steam plows, aquatic railroads, and fire-proof houses. In 1832, he made the utterly delusional claim that "my illustrations of 30 years' travels, with 2,000 figures will soon begin to be published, and be superior to those of my friend Audubon." Although he published more than nine hundred titles in his lifetime, he was utterly ignored and forgotten at the time of his death of cancer in 1840. His landlord locked the corpse in his room, intending to sell it to a medical school, until a small group of friends broke in, lowered it by ropes out the back window, and spirited it away for burial in the "Strangers Ground" of Ronaldson's cemetery. In the words of one biographer, he "loved no man or woman, and died, as he had lived, alone." When sold at auction, his lifetime's collection of books and specimens, filling eight drays, left his administrator $14.43 in debt.

It could be argued that Audubon's abuse of the laws of hospitality – his cruel pranks played upon a trusting and vulnerable guest – had a tangible negative impact on the progress of American science and naturalism. While such a claim is debatable and may even be grandiloquent, in my opinion it barely scratches the surface of the enormity of Audubon's crime.

The story is told in Judges of the traveling Levite who, on his way from Bethlehem to Ephraim, is given shelter by an old farmer of Gibeah. That evening, the Benjaminites of Gibeah surround the farmer's house and demand that he deliver the Levite to them. Rather than violate the law of hospitality requiring hosts to protect their guests, the farmer offers the mob his own virgin daughter. In the end, the thugs take the Levite's concubine, whom they rape and murder, an outrage that precipitates a war and the desolation of the tribe of Benjamin.

The farmer of Gibeah knew very well that there was more at stake in protecting his guest than his own honor and the safety of a single traveler. This was a time when the Israelites were consolidating their power over recently and imperfectly conquered land. If they could not guarantee safe travel among their own kind, how could they ever hope to establish secure and prosperous dominion? Hospitality was not just a revered tradition – it was also an essential component of national unity and the trading network. Its failure posed a direct threat to Israelite strength. Ensuring safe and comfortable passage to one's kinsmen was a patriotic duty.

Americans and Europeans on the American frontier in the early nineteenth century were in a very similar situation. Frontiers may be opened by force, but they can only coalesce and mature around communities, which must be prepared to welcome newcomers into their midst. White people who found themselves on the frontier without kinfolk had no choice but to rely on the hospitality of strangers, as there were no hotels, inns, or even reliable roads to speak of and federal currency was scarce. Audubon, who played long-term host to several frontier families, knew this better than most. Unless the newcomers could trust their hosts implicitly, they would not come, or stay, so reliable hospitality was as crucial to the consolidation of frontiers as armed self-defense. What Audubon did, for better or for worse, in failing in his duties as a host was to put the entire vanguard of American westward expansion at risk. The fact that Rafinesque may not have been the easiest of guests, or that Audubon's pranks might be considered by some to be well-earned payback, is no excuse whatsoever.

But we do not need to embrace the political argument to condemn Audubon for *lèse hospitalité*. On the face of it, true, he assumed his responsibility for feeding and housing a stranger in need, but that can hardly mitigate his delinquency. What he did was to take in a stranger – some sort of holy fool by all appearances – gain his trust and friendship, and then betray him in the cruelest and most unjustified way. Why did he do it? For fun? Rafinesque certainly didn't need anybody's help making a fool of himself. Out of boredom, pique, rivalry? We will probably never know, but it hardly matters. Abusing a guest under one's own roof undermines the entire edifice of hospitality, which perches at the best of times on dubious foundations. Without trust, there is no hospitality; without hospitality, there is no civilization; without civilization, there are no naturalists.

CHAPTER IV

THE DUCHESS WHO WOULDN'T SIT DOWN

People of quality know everything without ever having had to learn a thing.

Molière, *Les Précieuses ridicules*

When I was a young boy, I had a friend from a wealthy and very proper French family. His father was the first secretary in the embassy or perhaps even the ambassador to the Court of St. James. My friend was the kind of child who cried when he got a B+. His brother and very beautiful older sister were the same. It was a family of brilliant, brittle overachievers with very high standards. I didn't know such people existed and I was wholly unprepared when I was invited for a sleepover.

I am grateful for being unable to remember most of that awful night, but I do remember the supper. The table in the formal dining room was clothed in white linen and set with crystal, silver, and bone china. We sat bolt upright, leaning our forearms delicately against the table's edge. My friend's father sat at the far end, wearing a crisp gray suit. His mother sat at the opposite end with her back to a hotplate on which our supper awaited, a small silver bell by her right hand. She gave it the most peremptory tinkle and the maidservant wafted in from the kitchen to serve us.

The meal was something revolting to me at the time – sweetbreads or pigeon in aspic. Whatever it was, it provoked my friend and me into making surreptitious grimaces of disgust at each other across the table. This was inappropriate behavior; my friend knew it, but I didn't (it would have seemed perfectly normal, even restrained, in my home). I persisted and was reprimanded with an icy stare from Madame. My friend's sister was in the middle of telling a story of heartbreak or academic difficulties. I grew nervous, flustered, and overcome by hysterical giggling, which I managed to suppress only partway through her account, so that, when I could contain myself no longer, it appeared that I was mocking her suffering. I was asked to leave the table and finished my supper in the kitchen, with the maid. The sister never talked to me again. I wet the bed that night. I was not invited back.

It is an ugly but undeniable truth that everybody has someone they can't invite to the party. Quirky traits and tics that may be endearing to or at least accepted by a friend suddenly become awkward and embarrassing when that friend is a host. We may love this eccentric dearly and enjoy an intimate and confiding friendship with her, but she just doesn't know how to behave in company. She talks about herself obsessively, she is easily offended by offhand remarks, she is too loud, she is too quiet, she is suspicious of strangers, she is too aggressive, she is too picky an eater. We think twice about inviting her, this old and loyal friend of ours. Can she really be trusted to keep her temper? Will she really fit in this group? Who can we sit her next to? *Does she understand the rules?*

Maybe the truth is simpler. Maybe she understands the rules perfectly well but just can't be bothered to obey them. There is, after all – as I remember very well – a certain perverse satisfaction in wetting the bed, especially someone else's.

In 1648, France was engulfed in a four-year civil war known as the Fronde. The conflict began as a revolt of the Parlement against the king's powers of taxation, but was later complicated by the ambitions to power of a cabal of aristocrats led by the prince de Condé, a noble of the highest lineage and cousin to the Dauphin Louis. When Condé was arrested, his supporters rose up. The prince was released and Chief Minister Mazarin dismissed, but Louis's mother, Anne of Austria, succeeded in dividing Condé's party and he was indicted again in 1651, leading to another uprising in which the prince successfully held Paris for a time. The royalists, led by the great General Turenne, eventually turned the tide and Condé fled to Spain. Louis, now king, returned to Paris in 1652 at the age of fourteen, and Mazarin was recalled shortly thereafter.

For the rest of the 1650s, as France warred with Spain, Louis spent his time much as any teenager would, to the extent possible for a king of France with the eyes of all Europe upon him. He stayed up late with his friends, danced a great deal, flirted scandalously with his brother's wife. A famously expert shot, he hunted tirelessly at his châteaux outside Paris – including a modest lodge built by his father in the small village of Versailles – and indulged an almost inexhaustible appetite for sex with the many willing ladies of the court, single and less so. Given the disarray of his finances, the corruption of state officials, and Mazarin's tight fist, his hospitality was necessarily limited, at least in comparison to what it would be a decade later, but he nevertheless managed to stage some memorable events, such as the great carousel of 1656, at which three teams of knights, Louis at the head of one in crimson and white and a plumed helmet, competed at spearing a golden ring.

Still, throughout this time Louis stayed close to Mazarin, absorbing his advice and eagerly learning the intricacies of statecraft and kingship. Mazarin could not live forever, and Louis had never forgotten the bitter lessons of the Fronde or his humiliation at the hands of the self-serving nobility, including his close relatives. He remembered only too well their greed and fickle allegiance; how he had been compelled for lack of funds to wear the same ratty dressing gown and sleep in the same worn sheets for three years straight; how, one night in 1651, he lay shivering in bed, feigning sleep, as his mother – in an effort to allay rumors that the royal family was planning to abandon Paris – had exhibited him to the mob that had entered the Palais Royal; how, when they did flee to Saint-Germain, he and his court had had to bed down on cots and straw in the empty, echoing palace. Even at that tender age, Louis had held a deep conviction in his divine right, and his keen sense of the outrage done then to his person and his position was in no way blunted by a carefree adolescence – nor, indeed, by the subsequent decades of unparalleled glory. It had been the kind of childhood that breaks most people and tempers a very few, providing them both with their obsessions and with the strength and will to pursue them.

In 1659, a peace treaty was signed with Spain, ending twenty-four years of war, and ratified the following year with Louis's marriage to the infanta Marie-Thérèse. In 1661, Mazarin died and Louis assumed full control of the government, declining to replace the chief minister. That same year, Louis ordered the arrest and trial of Nicolas Fouquet, his superintendant of finances, on corruption charges. He hired the now unemployed trio of geniuses who had built Fouquet's château at Vaux – the architect Le Vau, the painter Le Brun, and the landscaper Le Nôtre – and set them to rebuilding his hunting lodge at Versailles.

It is not clear how long Louis had been planning to make Versailles the crucible of his experiment in autodeification, but he had certainly been toying with the idea long before Mazarin's death. It had always been his favorite house, while the Louvre had the double disadvantage of being far too small, capable of housing a bare few hundred courtiers, and of being in central Paris, vulnerable to the mob. Shortly before his arrest, Fouquet had been foolish enough to host a fête at Vaux that was so lavish – entertainment by Molière, music by Lully, poetry by La Fontaine – as to throw his financial and cultural superiority over the king into stark relief to everyone present, and it may have marked the decisive indignity that sealed Louis's determination. In any case, with the establishment of peace and the speedy regularization of his finances, Louis was now free to turn his very focused attention to building his dream home and mapping out a system that would transform Versailles into the most luxurious and escape-proof gilded cage ever conceived, and to forge his hospitality at Versailles into the ultimate tool of authoritarian government.

From 1651 onward, Louis was the sole source of power and advancement. Shutting out the entire noble estate, including his own brother, he appointed only commoners to his tiny council, and then only to advise – never, under any circumstances, to take decisions. Every significant preferment, every sinecure, every military appointment, every grant, and every loan – even minor matters once lucratively assigned to venal undersecretaries – now went directly through him. It is true that Louis worked harder, and enjoyed his work more, than any French monarch had before him, but he devised a relatively simple basis on which to make his decisions. If the king were to give you anything, he had to know you and to like you, both by reputation and by sight. And in order to know you, he had to see you every day – in his hallways, at his games, in his bedroom, in the chapel, at his entertainments. For any nobleman with even a modicum of ambition, attendance upon the king was virtually compulsory.

When the court had been in the capital, every nobleman had kept his own town house, along with his privacy, within easy reach of the palace. This was no longer possible. Versailles the village offered no suitable lodgings and Paris, some fourteen miles away, was too far for a daily commute. The château itself had apartments for some one thousand courtiers and ancillary lodgings for four thousand of their attendants, but the competition for quarters there was fierce, despite the fact that it was notoriously drafty and cold in the winter. Family apartments, handed down from one generation to the next, were usually subdivided, sometimes into tiny airless cubicles with barely enough room for a cot and a chamber pot. Since the ceilings were so high, the larger apartments were often divided horizontally as well, creating two floors of cramped, smoky, windowless warrens hidden behind a pair of magnificent gilded doors on a main corridor.

Still, as the duc de Saint-Simon discovered to his chagrin, "to live at the Court without a lodging, or even to frequent it, was intolerable and impossible." He sums up the dilemma common to every courtier: "The care of my patrimony required my constant presence at the Court, for there would always be the possibility of its being removed from me in anger." When, through carelessness, he loses the reversion of his apartment to his own brother-in-law, he finds himself in despair.

> The greatest trouble for me . . . was that I had no lodging at Versailles, for not only did that entail the fatigue of journeys to and from Paris, but it curtailed the social activities that imperceptibly brought one great advantage.

"I never see him," the king would say of an absentee courtier, and it was not meant, and never taken, as a casual remark. It was an almost certain forewarning that, some time in the not-too-distant future, the king would strip the delinquent of his reversions, his command, or his hereditary post, all of which had to be paid for and renewed at intervals. The doomed man would find his friends melting away, his invitations evaporating, his reputation sullied. He would soon have little option but to slink off to his provincial estates, his career and social prospects gone, to mingle with the lowly local gentry, the *"bonne noblesse,"* a term he would have used at court not long before with utmost contempt. There was no recourse, no appeal. Louis was a stubborn and opinionated arbiter – though he often bought his opinions wholesale from the mistresses and courtiers who had his ear – and he rarely reversed a bias once he had made it known. "His Majesty does not like you," Turenne told one disconsolate courtier, "and when he has a poor impression of someone he never sets it aside." Even more rarely did the king find himself compelled by public opinion to tolerate someone he actively disliked, such as the charming prince de Conti, whom "the courtiers could not easily dispense with." Louis ultimately made an exception in the case of Conti (who was, after all, his own grandson), but "was much relieved when he died."

The painful issue of lodgings was a problem surpassed only by that of financing a life at court. Versailles was prohibitively expensive for all but the wealthiest aristocrats, making regular attendance, with its potential for securing favor, pensions, and appointments, all the more necessary. Since most Versailles residents spent their days either attending the king or roaming the hallways and gardens, appearances had to be kept up at all costs. The burden of keeping servants, stables, and carriages; travel and entertainment expenses; the constant gambling and gift giving; and, above all, the cost of clothing and wigs, kept many on the verge of penury and in hopeless debt. Costumes, of the finest silk, gold, and silver thread, with buttons and jewelry of the most precious metals and gemstones, were changed several times a day. The king was said to dress "in utmost simplicity" – he hardly ever wore his diamond-encrusted coat worth twelve million livres – but when he ordered new clothes he was likely to set off a near riot of shopping among his courtiers. The wedding of Louis's grandson, the duc de Bourgogne, to Marie-Adelaïde of Savoy set Saint-Simon back twenty thousand livres (about ninety thousand dollars) in clothing costs and established a standard in rapacious rivalry for tailors that even the king had cause to rue.

This, of course, was all as Louis intended. It served several of his purposes. First, it made his the most glittering court in Europe, concentrating all the country's wealth and glamour in one place. Then, too, since the grounds and staterooms of Versailles were open to any decently dressed member of the public, it provided a show for the masses, dazzling them with the glory of France, filling them with patriotic pride and awe of their sovereign. Above all, however, was the dependency of the nobility. Poor courtiers were submissive courtiers, far from the power and the financial bases in the provinces that had under-written their earlier rebellions. If the haughtiest and most belli-gerent *Frondeurs*, such as Condé and the duc de Beaufort, could now be seen trotting abjectly down the Hall of Mirrors at Louis's heels; and with rich, less rich, and heavily indebted alike engaged in heated sartorial competition with one another, instead of in intrigues and cabals; and with the entire court a fishbowl under Louis's watchful eye, "discovering the most secret views of our own courtiers, their most hidden interests which come to us through the play of contrary interests," who was there left in all of France to rise up and challenge the regal authority? No one, that's who.

The beauty of it was that Louis had no need to enforce his will through terror. On the contrary, any nobleman favored enough by birth or talent to be a member of the Sun King's court counted himself among the most fortunate beings on earth. Anxious though they might be over money and social advancement, very few courtiers had any more sense of being put upon, suppressed, or manipulated by their sovereign than do the angels in heaven. Like anyone who has ever given away something that cannot be retrieved, they were perfectly thrilled to be able to live in the comforting fiction that what they had lost was of little value.

It goes without saying, though, that Louis gave his courtiers scant leisure or motivation to dwell on this side of things. He knew that they must be entertained and distracted, given the long hours of enforced idleness between public functions, and that he himself was the principal source of entertainment. His life, accordingly, was played out almost entirely in public, from the moment he awoke at eight-thirty A.M. to some one hundred noblemen milling in his bedchamber, separated from the royal bed by nothing more than a wooden barrier; through the supposedly private family meals and the public *grands couverts*, during which throngs hung anxiously goggling at every sip of the royal broth; to his ritual *couchée* at eleven-thirty P.M., an equally crowded event.

His love life, too, was a matter of public record, the position of titular mistress being formally recognized and compensated. He cheated openly on his mistresses, who were not always as tolerant as the queen. Each of his three official mistresses – Louise de la Vallière, the marquise de Montespan, and Mme de Maintenon – was eased in and out of his favor with an exquisitely slow and painful deliberateness that kept the court gossips (i.e., everyone) keen-eyed and limber-tongued for years. When he eventually took Mme de Maintenon as his lover, he housed her in rooms directly behind those of Montespan, to whose royal bastards she had once been governess. By appearing to enter Montespan's apartment, only to slip out the back into Maintenon's, the king was in principle protecting her feelings and prerogatives, but since everyone at court knew all about the ruse, he was in fact undermining and serving her up as a rather corpulent sacrifice to court scandal. In the same way, when he humiliated the hapless Maréchal de Gramont – by first reading him a madrigal, which he encouraged the old man to disparage, and then revealing it as his own – it was most certainly in full view and earshot of dozens of idle rumormongers. Dainty titillations went a long way at Versailles when tendered by the king.

The members of his family were expected to assume their share of the burden of public life. The king's brother, known in court as Monsieur, made no attempt to conceal his passion for the handsome and callow chevalier de Lorraine, on whose behalf he begged Louis for the reversion of two abbeys. When the king refused, Monsieur left the court in a huff – Olivier Bernier points out that Louis XIII's brother would have started a civil war in similar circumstances – and the chevalier was clapped in jail. Humbled, Monsieur came crawling back and, when the chevalier was released, collapsed on the floor and embraced his brother's knees in gratitude. All this was played out on the public stage.

Not even the royal children were spared the host's responsibility to entertain. As one eyewitness noted of the duc de Bourgogne's wedding: "The new King [William III of England] has made his entry into London; the spectacle was very grand, but its expense is nothing when compared to the marriage." After the ceremony and mass, a sumptuous meal was served to the royal family at a great horseshoe-shaped table, which was followed by a game of cards, a fireworks display, and another banquet. Then the entire party, now joined by the recently deposed James II of England and his queen, trooped off to the newlyweds' bedchamber:

The duc de Bourgogne undressed himself in the anti-chamber, and the King of England presented him his shirt; the duchesse de Bourgogne undressed herself before all the ladies who were in her chamber, and the Queen of England presented her her chemise. As soon as the duchesse de Bourgogne was in bed, it was announced to the duc de Bourgogne, who got into bed upon the right side. The King and Queen of England retired. The King went to bed . . . The duchesse de Lude, and all the ladies of the duchesse de Bourgogne, remained around the bed, the curtains of which were undrawn all round . . . The duc de Beauvilliers, as governor of the duc de Bourgogne, remained by the bed-side while he was with the duchesse de Bourgogne.

The duke and new duchess were fifteen and twelve years old, respectively.

But even the travails and deflowerings of the royal family were not enough to keep the court quiescent and amused. Three times a week, the *soirées d'appartement* were held in the state apartments: beverages in the Abundance Salon, delicacies in the Venus Salon, dancing in the Mars Salon, gaming in the Mercury Salon, and music in the Apollo Salon. There was theater by Molière and Racine, music by Lully and Lalande. There were Le Nôtre's magnificent two thousand acres of parkland and gardens – reduced, sere, and dismal today by comparison – with some twelve miles of roads and paths; hundreds of potted orange trees; fifty fountains; fifty-five acres of canal plied by Venetian gondolas; the mysterious, eternally twilit Grotto of Thetis, now gone, and the Baths of Apollo; secluded alleys, groves, and hidden trysting nooks. There were billiards and hunting and the endless composition of billets-doux. And, of course, there was conversation: the refined, literate, vicious conversation that seemed to have continued unabated for generations; secretive conclaves in the corridors and stairwells; raucous outbursts in the gaming rooms; sweet plaintive pleadings in the trellised arbors; ghostly whispers in the galleries at dead of night – as inexhaustible, inescapable, and penetrating as the trickles, rivulets, and geysers of water pumped to every far corner of the vast estate.

But if all this still failed to distract the court – if, as Mme de Sévigné asserted, "the entertainments were to become boring by their very multiplicity" – the king could always pull off the miracle of a perfectly choreographed fête, such as that held on the night of July 18, 1668. Early in the evening, the king and queen set off for a stroll through the gardens, followed by some twelve hundred courtiers, all of whom were aware that something was afoot but had no idea of what it might be. As they turned a corner into a secluded alley, they came, almost as if by chance, upon a pentagonal structure made entirely of woven branches. Within, five tables were set with delicacies: one had been built up to resemble a mountain, its caverns filled with cold meats; another had become a palace, constructed entirely of marzipan and pastry; yet another was a pyramid of crystallized fruit; the others held vases of liqueurs and platters of caramels, all charmingly draped in flowers. Potted orange trees were hung with candied oranges, while, at the center of the structure, a thirty-foot fountain played. After the guests had refreshed themselves, the king set out in his barouche, the queen in her chaise, and the courtiers followed in carriages. They passed down a linden alley and came, again as if by magic, to a theater, with seating for two thousand, designed by Carlo Vigarani and erected in secret over the past several days. It was covered by greenery without, by tapestries within, and was lit by thirty-two crystal chandeliers hung from the rafters. The stage was flanked by columns of bronze and lapis. The play, a light pastoral comedy by Molière, was set in a garden, and the set designed to reveal the gardens behind, giving the impression that the entire park was present onstage. After the show, the company headed out once again, led by His Majesty, who knew just where he was going but managed to give the impression that he was following his whim. Next came ballet in an octagonal dance hall clad in marble and porphyry, an equally temporary structure thrown up in a secluded nook of the gardens. After another brief expedition, the company came upon an octagonal dining hall rampant with marble satyrs, dolphins, and gods. Fruit trees and flowers filled every available space. At the center of the room was a small mountain, crowned by a statue of Pegasus and enlivened by tumbling streams, surrounded by a circular table set for 450 guests, who chose from among 280 dishes. The rest of the group ate in side halls. Mme de Sévigné dined at the king's table, a moment she would never forget. As the *médianoche* wound down, the guests, always behind the king, began to wander back toward the château when suddenly the night exploded with fireworks. The first were set off at some distance away, highlighting the palace, but gradually they drew closer and closer until the company found itself entirely surrounded by jets of flame and sparks erupting from two hundred four-foot vases. When these died down, to the relief of many, it appeared that the evening had come to an end, but just then the Grotto of Thetis was set ablaze with Roman candles, the sky above it traced by rockets with Louis's double-*L* emblem. Timed to the very minute, the sun rose just as the last spark went out, and the king and queen set off for Saint-Germain in their carriage.

The fête had been pulled off at great expense, but that was hardly the point. The message that came through loud and clear was that this was something only the Sun King could ever hope to pull off. The mere fact that ten thousand workers had labored in total secrecy, practically under the very noses of the court, was nothing short of miraculous, but the true success lay in the way it had been designed to highlight Louis's absolute authority. He had only to turn a corner, serene and unabashed, for entire theaters, dance halls, and banquet halls to spring up in his path, mountains to rise, rivers to erupt. The very statues "seemed to dance and express their pleasure at being visited by such a great monarch attended by such a fine court." And the sun itself, "jealous of the perquisites of the night," kindly waits for the king's entertainments to end before showing itself. In all of Le Pautre's engravings of the evening, the king is always in the center foreground, his back to the viewer, at the heart of a throng and yet untouched and untouchable, entirely isolated in his glory.

What wouldn't you and I give to have been a member of that company and to bask in his presence? Since we weren't, we might tell ourselves that, tempting as it sounds, we wouldn't have given up our freedom for it. But imagine, just for the sake of argument, that it were possible. Imagine the thrill of receiving the most sought-after invitation, then multiply it a thousandfold, because this is not an evening's glory but a lifetime's, an eternity's. You are not visiting, you are at home, among your own, forever. Like being called to heaven, anything you need to let go of to get in is entirely expendable. Now what would you give? Is there any way in which you would fail or refuse to conform? What possible attraction could there be in dissidence?

To submit to the etiquette of Versailles was to abandon any pretense, however forlorn, at being a free agent. Your choice was stark and simple: give in or get out. In the king's house, you lived by the king's rules. Of course, Louis had not actually invented etiquette, but he did perfect its evolution as an exquisite straitjacket. At Versailles, you quite literally could not take a step, could not raise a spoon to your lips, could not powder your wig without first considering who you might offend and whether they were in a position to punish you for it. With all their real power gone, the nobles bickered and litigated with obsessive zeal over the infinite nuances of precedence. As Saint-Simon put it:

> He was conscious that the substantial favours he had to bestow were not nearly sufficient to produce a continual effect; he had therefore to invent imaginary ones, and no one was so clever in devising petty distinctions and preferences which aroused jealousy and emulation.

The king employed a full-time official whose sole function was to rule in disputes over whose carriage might pass first through a gate, who was allowed to step through a certain door ahead of whom. Mme de Sévigné relates an unseemly tussle between Mme de Gêvres and Mme d'Arpajon:

> Mme d'Arpajon was ahead of me. I thought Gêvres expected me to give her my place, but I owed her something from the other day, and I paid her back in full and didn't budge. Mademoiselle [the duchesse de Lorraine] was on her bed. So she was compelled to take her place at the bottom, below the dais – very annoying. Mademoiselle's drink was served and the serviette had to be offered. I spied Mme de Gêvres slipping her glove off her skinny hand. I nudged Mme d'Arpajon, who understood, took off her own glove and advanced a step, cut out Gêvres and took and offered the serviette. Gêvres was covered with shame and looked very sheepish.

In various forms, such silent struggles took place a thousand times a day at court, but it is certain that if the object of servility had been a son of France or the king instead of his niece, the serviette skirmish would have ended in dangerously bad blood, and perhaps bloodshed.

Of course, access to the king was strictly limited, as it was to varying degrees to all princes of the blood. The only place one was allowed to follow the king was in the park, and only the highest ranking nobleman in the bedchamber was privileged to hold His Majesty's candlestick at the *couchée*. Only the most exalted were permitted in the *ruelles* on either side of the bed.

But perhaps the strangest and most alien aspect of these rules was that governing the use of chairs. These rules were observed with a prissy obsessiveness that appears to us to border on perversity. If you were not fully versed in every nicety of seating etiquette – which was complicated by the fact that it was common to receive guests of inferior rank in bed – you could easily find yourself in trouble. When Louis welcomed the exiled James II to France and established him at Saint-Germain, saying "this is your home," Mme de Sévigné's very first thought was "I don't know how they will have arranged the princesses' chairs." One of the first things out of La Grange's mouth in the opening scene of Molière's *Les Précieuses ridicules* is "They could hardly bring themselves to ask us to sit down." And when Mademoiselle, heartbroken by the king's refusal to allow her to marry her one true love, actually invited Mme de Sévigné to kneel down beside her bed, it was as if every social barrier had been swept aside: "On this occasion," she confessed, "I have been through emotions one does not often feel for people of such rank."

There were four basic types of seat at court and you had to know precisely when and if you were allowed to occupy them, and in whose presence. Except when no member of the direct royal family was present, only the king and queen were permitted to sit in armchairs. When Louis sat Mme de Maintenon in an armchair in the presence of his grandchildren, it was a clear signal that, as many had suspected, he had finally married her (in such secrecy that, to this day, the date of the marriage is uncertain). Grandchildren of France (that is, those of the king and Monsieur) were also allowed the armchair if no one of higher rank, including their own parents, was present.

Next in prestige below the armchair was the straight-backed, armless chair, which was permitted to princes and princesses of the blood, cardinals, duchesses, foreign princes, and consorts of Spanish grandees, but only in the presence of grandchildren of France or their inferiors. When Monsieur asked his brother to allow Madame to occupy a chair in the presence of the queen, the king refused point-blank, explaining, "I did not think I should ever allow anything that would bring him too close [in rank] to me."

Next came the *tabouret*, a low stool with fixed legs. Dukes, foreign princes, Spanish grandees, and noblewomen took the *tabouret* in the presence of grandchildren of France, but lesser nobles had to stand. In the presence of the dauphin (the crown prince) and his wife, and of the children of France (the sons and daughters of the king and Monsieur), the grandchildren of France, princesses of the blood, cardinals, duchesses, foreign princesses, and the consorts of Spanish grandees took the *tabouret*, while all others stood. In the presence of the king and queen, only the dauphin, dauphine, children and grandchildren of France, princesses of the blood, duchesses, foreign princesses, and consorts of Spanish grandees could take the *tabouret*. Cardinals, too, were permitted the *tabouret*, but only if the king were absent. All others stood. In other circumstances, courtiers were also allowed to sit on *ployants* (folding stools) and *placets* (cushions) on the floor.

By far the most contentious of these seats was the *tabouret* – Mme de Sévigné calls it the "sacred *tabouret*" – because the categories assigned to it were somewhat fluid. One could never *become* the sovereign or his direct descendant, but one could be *made* a duchess. To "take the *tabouret*" meant to assume one's rank at court, like Balzac's heroine:

> The duchesse de Langeais, a Navarreine by birth, came of a ducal house which had made a point of never marrying below its rank since the reign of Louis XIV. Every daughter of the house must sooner or later take a *tabouret*.

The other wonderful thing about a *tabouret* was that one could earn it. One of the many perks of being the king's lover was the very real opportunity of being offered a *tabouret* when he had finished with you. Since, with the unique exception of Mme de Maintenon, it was a near certainty that he *would* finish with you sooner or later, it may well be that the *tabouret*, which would last a lifetime, was anticipated not as a consolation prize but as the ultimate goal of the transaction. Consider one lucky castoff, Mme de Fontanges:

> Mme de Fontanges is a duchess with an income of 20,000 écus; today she was receiving compliments on her day-bed. The King went there openly. She takes her official stool tomorrow and then goes to spend Easter in an abbey the King has presented to one of her sisters. This is a kind of separation that will pay homage to his confessor's severity. Some people say that this establishment smacks of dismissal. I don't really believe it, but time will show.

Time did show – it was a dismissal.

The downside to the *tabouret*'s accessibility was that it was possible to believe that one was entitled to it when one was not. In

1704, the duke of Mantua surrendered his duchy to Louis rather than have it ravaged in the course of the Italian war. Louis reciprocated by inviting the duke to Versailles, where he was received with the highest honors of a foreign prince. These included being called "cousin" by the king, being allowed to drive his carriage into the great courtyards of the Louvre and Versailles, and even being presented to the duchesse de Bourgogne in her *ruelle*. When he died shortly thereafter, his widow retired to a convent but soon bored of it and made the decision to present herself at court. Since she was a Lorraine and drew a court pension, and since her mother was close to Mme de Maintenon, and since her late husband had done Louis a considerable service, she had good reason to anticipate a royal reception.

> She arrived . . . with every intention of adopting rank equal to that of a Granddaughter of France, that is to say offering her hand and an armchair to no one, no matter who they were [save King and Queen], and not accompanying visitors one step towards the door.

The first sign that her ambitions were misplaced emerged during a visit to the widow of the Maréchal de Bellefonds. She was "so dumbfounded to find herself offered only a *ployant* that she sat down; but when her senses returned somewhat later, she left and never again set foot inside the door." Residing at the château de Vincennes, she soon found herself twiddling her thumbs for lack of titled callers. It turns out, as only the duchess of Mantua was unaware, that Mme de Maintenon was in a "disobliging mood" and that the king, rankled by the intrigues of the Lorraines, "had no wish to give the Duchess any special place at court." He ordered that she present herself at Versailles in morning dress, thereby making it impossible for her to attend any function at which full court dress was required. This proved to be a fatal snub to her pretensions.

The indignities, every one a matter of seating, piled up fast and furious. At Versailles, the king refused to kiss her and remained standing (thus preventing her from taking a seat of any kind), as did the king's grandsons. Within fifteen minutes, she was dismissed and sent back to Vincennes, where she continued to be visited by no one.

Mme d'Elbeuf [her mother], who was not so easily discouraged, next tried to obtain for her a chair with a back in Mme la Duchesse de Bourgogne's drawing-room. Now the wives and daughters of reigning princes, whose ministers are recognized by all the courts of Europe, were traditionally offered chairs with backs at the late queen's receptions, but for the first visit only; thenceforward they had only *tabourets* like any one else, and no different from the French duchesses. The Duchess of Mecklenburg was granted this privilege, but the Duchess of Mantua was not, although her mother asked for it on four separate occasions.

Rather than accept a *tabouret*, which she considered beneath her dignity, the duchess of Mantua chose not to sit at all, and never returned to court. Instead, she moved to Paris, where she expected her rank to be appreciated. Again she was wrong. She ran into trouble almost immediately when she challenged the right of the prince and princesse de Montbazon's coach to precede hers through the second gate of the Palais Royal. When neither side agreed to back down, a brawl erupted between the coachmen, M. de Montbazon threatening to thrash anyone who touched his horses. Eventually, it was discovered that the two coaches might just squeeze through at the same time, and bloodshed was averted, but the scandal did nothing to improve the duchess's prospects.

She soon came to see that haughtiness was getting her nowhere. She changed her tone, paying visits without waiting to receive a first call, "driving like anyone else in a two-horse coach." She offered her armchairs freely and even conducted most ladies as far as the door. Her newfound humility was a hit; the duchesse de Lauzun broke the ice with a first visit and society followed. It was decidedly not court society, but it was better than nothing. She began to throw fashionable card parties, the ultimate acknowledgment that her position was irreparable.

> Her grandiose aspirations to royal rank melted away and all her schemes for being great at Court were succeeded by the ambition to be a good hostess in Paris.

She might have convinced Saint-Simon of that, but she couldn't convince herself. She was dead within the year at age twenty-five, presumably of a broken heart.

If the duchess of Mantua had agreed in 1709 to take a stool instead of insisting on a chair, all her social setbacks could have been avoided. But she understood every bit as well as the king that there was far more at stake than sore knees and dusty hems – even at the cost of her own public humiliation, she was determined to uphold the order that had secured everything she and her family possessed: wealth, rank, reputation, tradition, and continuity. As the king himself put it:

> Those who think that ambitions of this kind are mere affairs of ceremonial are wholly deluded; there is nothing in these matters which does not request careful thought or which is

not capable of having serious consequences. The people whom we rule . . . judge according to what they see on the outside, so that it is most usually by the place and rank that they measure their respect and their obedience.

By refusing to sit down in the king's house, the duchess was not bucking the reigning ideology, but in fact acting out a cruel obeisance to it.

Almost everyone did, from Vatel, the prince de Condé's chef, who stabbed himself through the heart rather than serve the king an unworthy meal; to the duc d'Antin, who, at his château Petit-Bourg, made a precise replica of Mme de Maintenon's rooms at Saint Cyr, down to the very way her books were stacked on the table. Upon a visit from Louis XIV, d'Antin had an entire avenue of chestnut trees silently uprooted overnight, as the king slept, rather than obstruct His Majesty's view at breakfast. You do what you have to do. Or, at least, most of us do.

But there is always the rare individual who just has to dissent, regardless of all the seductive inducements to conformity. They just can't help themselves, the impulse to self-assertion is too strong. They just have to wet the bed, so to speak. In Louis XIV's Versailles, self-assertion meant, at great peril, refusing the king's hospitality. Not many had the guts or the imagination for it, but there was one. Not only did this man manage to slip the shackles of the king's hospitality; he also actually managed to raise, from the depths of a perverse and tormented imagination, an alternate universe in which he stood the entire concept of hospitality as ideology on its head and, ultimately, made it work to his own advantage. He didn't really want it this way; if you had asked him, he probably would have claimed to prefer a life of ease and privilege. He just couldn't help himself. With Roger de Rabutin, comte de Bussy, more so than with most, character really was destiny.

The portraits of Bussy reveal a dashing cavalier straight out of central casting for *The Three Musketeers*, with his roguish moustache, voluminous wig and gleaming armor, flouncy collar, and wicked smile. In fact, he was all that and more, everything you might expect from such an archetype: a womanizer and adulterer, a willful malingerer, a sardonic wit, inconstant in love and allegiance, a boisterous carouser who usually let his high spirits lead him into indiscretion. He was also a fine writer with a keen eye for telling detail and social power relationships. He was lucky enough to have been born into precisely the wrong century, the one time and place where all his charms and weaknesses were sure to set him apart to his advantage and great peril. A century earlier and he would have been just another swashbuckler in Henri IV's court of scoundrels; a century later and he probably would have ended up sharing a cell with the marquis de Sade.

He was born in 1618, the third son of a Burgundian nobleman of ancient lineage, and extremely well educated by the Jesuits. His father sent him off to war under Turenne at the age of sixteen, where he shamelessly deserted his first command, though his youth saved him from any unpleasant repercussions. Almost from the onset, plagued by a lack of money to buy a commission, he began writing poetry to make his reputation in society. In 1638, his father transferred his own colonel's commission to him and Louis XIII gave him twelve thousand livres to buy recruits, which he promptly lost. He was a typical young officer, fighting bravely in the summer, loving too well in the off-season, dueling and brawling over women, one of whom, to his distress, turned out to be a beautiful hermaphrodite. His first stay in the Bastille, a mere five months, came in 1641, when he abandoned his troops to pursue a lover and his leaderless men went on a rampage of rape and pillage in the village of Moulins. Bussy quit the service.

Despite his clear avowal that "I despise marriage because I am the enemy of all constraint," he went on to marry his wealthy cousin Gabrielle de Toulongeon in 1643 and embarked on his first extramarital affair two years later. Racked with guilt, he stayed at home and moped as the French army went on to a glorious victory at Nördlingen in Flanders. In 1645, having outlived all five of his brothers, he inherited the title of comte de Bussy and went on to fight well with the duc d'Enghien (the future prince de Condé) in Catalonia, but he abandoned him after the defeat of Lérida. In 1648, he misguidedly kidnapped a rich widow whom he was convinced wanted desperately to be ravished.

He fought with Condé during the Fronde, participating in the siege of Paris, where he was taken prisoner for six hours. When Condé turned against Louis XIV, Bussy's allegiance to the sovereign caused a vague irritation to his conscience. He briefly considered switching sides but soon came to see that his only chance of getting paid was to stick with the prince, who eventually gave him only half of what he thought he was owed. Enough was enough: like his fellow *Frondeur* Cyrano de Bergerac, he went over to the king.

It was a good move. By thirty-five, he was lieutenant general in the light cavalry and gaining glory on the field and in the salons, where his witty contemporary portraits in meter and verse were much admired. The expression *rabutinade*, still current today, was coined to commemorate his clever wordplay. But Bussy was not the kind of man to press his advantages by cultivating the powerful; he was constitutionally unable to compel his instincts and his ambitions to cooperate with one another. He just couldn't keep his mouth shut or his pen civil. "All chivalry is extinct at court," he tactfully wrote about the dubious mores of the day, "but that is rather the fault of the ladies than of the knights." Of the powerful duchesse de Longueville, he simply said, "She was dirty and smelled bad." In a letter Bussy wrote to his first cousin Mme de Sévigné – and letters in those days had a way of finding a public readership – he described the ugliness of Condé in some detail. Condé, in turn, "would not suffer [Bussy] to walk the streets of Paris while he was there." It was to Bussy that Turenne had said, "His Majesty does not like you."

But all this would have amounted to little more than a stunted military career if Bussy had not continually pushed the envelope of good taste and restraint. In 1658, when Mme de Sévigné's husband had an affair with the famous courtisan Ninon de Lenclos, Bussy urged her to retaliate by committing adultery with himself, her own cousin; her refusal propelled him to write a caustic portrait in which he described her physical defects and accused her of inconstancy and frigidity. The next year, he became embroiled in the Roissy scandal, in which a notorious group of libertines, including a number of known homosexuals, spent a debauched and well-publicized weekend during Holy Week composing and reading filthy poetry about the king and his court. Mazarin exiled Bussy for fifteen months.

It was at this time that, to distract himself, he began composing the stories that would eventually become the *Histoires amoureuses des Gaules*, a licentious and libelous look at the loose morals of the Fronde in which the king appears as Théodose, Condé as Tyridate, and Mazarin as the Great Druid. The book was offered as a private gift to his lover, the marquise de Montglas, and passed about discreetly, apparently even amusing His Majesty. But Bussy made the mistake of lending it to the notoriously indiscreet marquise de la Baume, who was languishing in the convent where her husband had imprisoned her for her shamelessness. The marquise only had the book in her possession for forty-eight hours, but somehow managed to have it copied in its entirety. The copy eventually found its way to Holland, where it was published in 1665. In April of that year, three months after he had been inducted into the Académie française – two after the opening of Molière's *Don Juan* – Bussy was arrested by direct order of the king and imprisoned in the Bastille. Mme de Montglas promptly abandoned him and Mme de Sévigné refused to visit (although he drew on her essential good nature to repair their relationship later on). His health broken, he was released thirteen months later and exiled indefinitely to his estates in Burgundy.

Banishment was a relatively common form of punishment in those days. It might be difficult for us to discern the punitive factor in being compelled to live in splendor on a country estate, spared the enormous expense and stress of life at court, waited upon by an army of servants, and surrounded by the comforts and calm of home, were we not already aware of the unparalleled advantages of life as the guest of the king. Montaigne had lived happily and productively in self-exile, but few had his acquirements. Banishment was simply social death, the end of all ambition and glory, at least for most people. But Bussy was not most people. He soon resigned himself to the fact that this was not to be a short-term exile and embarked on a project that would prove to be unique in the annals of hospitality.

In the mid-seventeenth century, the only regular mail delivery in France was the thrice-weekly post between Paris and Dijon, some thirty miles from Bussy-le-Grand. Bussy took full advantage of it, launching an epic letter-writing campaign that would result in one of the most glorious correspondences of the century, including many vainly ingratiating pleas to the king and at least 155 letters to Mme de Sévigné. Other correspondents included the famous *précieuses* Mme de Scudéry and Mme Bossuet. He begged them all for news, gossip, and literary exchanges, and they obliged; over the eighteen years of his exile, despite his distance, Bussy became known as a reliable and discerning cultural arbiter, an "oracle" according to one admirer. Charpentier, dean of the Académie, wrote, "We often speak of you, citing the authority of your thoughts and words." He championed the poets Benserade and La Fontaine, and new members of the Académie often sent him their work for his lucid commentaries. In exile – far from the center of power, far from the glories of the court, far from the rigid constraints of the ruling ideology – Bussy seemed to find himself for the first time and attained a level of respect and admiration that had eluded him through decades of public life. Beginning in 1668, he would edit, condense, and reshape the information contained in his correspondence into his *Memoirs*, which he hoped to present to the king as a glorification of his epoch. He was genuinely disappointed when Louis chose Racine and Bossuet as his official biographers.

From almost the moment he landed back at home, Bussy had set about a grand remodeling of his château, Bussy-Rabutin, which is still considered among the finest in Burgundy. Every time he opened a correspondence with a new interlocutor, he begged them for a portrait of themselves, "for I wish to have you in my chambers as well as in my heart." He soon had an enormous collection (not necessarily of the highest quality), which he arranged in distinct galleries, each with its own portrait of himself hung prominently at the center. In the *Salle des devises* he hung paintings of the most glorious châteaux of France, interspersed with allegorical emblems pointedly highlighting the guiding vanities of his self-regard ("Noble in his noble origins"; "His ardor makes me bold"; "I bend but do not break"; "I stoop to rise"). In the *Salle des hommes de guerre* he hung sixty-five portraits of the great military leaders of France from the Hundred Years War to the Fronde. In the *Tour dorée* he hung portraits, each accompanied by witty and often sardonic commentary, of the most beautiful women of the court, including that of his former lover the marquise de Montglas: "The most beautiful mistress of the realm, she would have been the most lovable if she had not been the most faithless." The *Salon des belles-amies* featured the royal mistresses of the Valois and Bourbon dynasties, while another gallery held portraits of the kings of France, statesmen, and men of letters – including, of course, his own. His bedroom held portraits of twenty-two family members, including that of Mme de Sévigné and her daughter, Mme de Grignan.

In this way, Bussy re-created and surrounded himself with every facet of the society and its illustrious members he had left behind. He made himself, in a sense, host to all society. Given the effort he put into it (these galleries can still be seen today, more or less unchanged), it must have been a powerful comfort to him. It was also a lure, as many – including a number of courtiers who would not have been seen dead with Bussy on one of his rare clandestine visits to Paris – journeyed long and uncomfortable distances to see for themselves this by now famous simulacrum of their own world deep in the heart of the provinces. And there can be no doubt that his galleries gave him far more pleasure than the company of the dull and unlettered local gentry – the dreaded *bonne noblesse*.

"A man of good sense can build himself a Paris anywhere," he wrote. His was a Paris of the mind, the only kind where a misfit like Bussy was ever likely to be tolerated and entertained. Although no one has ever suggested that Bussy had any screws loose, it is not a great stretch to imagine him wandering his empty hallways, much as he had once strolled through the galleries of Versailles, making refined conversation and formulating nasty asides with all of his admiring peers, who, for once, were in little danger of reporting his indiscretions.

Bussy was eventually recalled by the king in 1682, but his return to court was far from triumphant. At Saint-Germain,

Louis allowed him to embrace his knees, but the long-sought pension was not forthcoming. Bussy waited five months, increasingly aware of being a dinosaur, then returned to Burgundy for good, where he edited his correspondence and, almost unbelievably, found God. He died in 1693 and his correspondence, published four years later, proved enormously popular. It went through fourteen editions in forty years and included the first-ever publication of letters by Mme de Sévigné. Among a number of works that appeared posthumously was an essay dating all the way back to 1649, titled *Discourse on Putting Adversity to Good Use*.

There is a relatively simple moral in the triangle of conflicting world views held by Louis XIV, the duchess of Mantua, and Roger de Bussy. The rules of social life are pegged to a sliding scale of necessary compromises, and every decision we make is, to some extent, informed by our willingness to conform to the expectations others have of us. We can allow ourselves to be tractable or obdurate, as we see fit and depending on circumstances. Our decision to act one way or the other will ultimately be based on the relative benefits of the outcome. This holds equally true for guests and for hosts.

But what happens when we must deal with people to whom these rules are meaningless, who are incapable of flexibility or compromise, such as the three main protagonists of this chapter? Because hospitality is all about control, when things go sour it tends to bring out the worst in everyone, perfectionists and rebels alike, turning hosts into tyrants and eccentrics into dissidents. We all know at least one person – an overly formal host or an antisocial guest – who will not or cannot alter his or her behavior to accommodate the comfort level of others. Do we engage such misfits in a battle of wills, seeking to bend them against their natures and insisting that they conform to our standards when they are under our roof, or do we allow our guests to be themselves, even when their selves are prickly, aggressive, or unsociable? If you are an intolerant host who imposes rules of behavior, the danger of creating dissidents in your midst – people who are constitutionally or temperamentally compelled to forgo your hospitality – is quite real. If, on the other hand, you allow your guests free rein to act out their idiosyncrasies, you risk undermining the control that, as we have seen, is so crucial to good hospitality.

It is a fine wire to walk. It is also just as pertinent to someone hosting a modest dinner party on a Saturday night as it is to any autocrat in a powdered wig. If, like Louis XIV, we play tyrant as host, we can afford to be as inflexible as we wish. Most of us would be glad to be shot of the duchess of Mantua but, unlike Louis, very sorry to lose the company of Roger de Bussy. Since we are more likely to be forced into the role of host as tyrant, however, we may find ourselves compelled to compromise. We may have to admit a few stuffy duchesses if we wish to retain our Bussys. In weighing the degree of control that we will be willing to exert over our guests, we will inevitably have to ask ourselves this question: Is one Bussy worth a house full of duchesses who won't sit down?

CHAPTER V

THE COCKENTRICE

And as for the Dwkys coort, as of lords & ladys & gentylwomen knyts, sqwyers & gentylmen I hert never of non lyek to it save King Artourys cort.

John Paston, letter from Bruges, 1468

My wife and I both work at jobs that are demanding and intellectually stimulating, but comparatively low-paying. Anywhere else in the country we might be considered very well off, but there is nowhere else in the country that we could practice our professions. In New York City, we get by. When it comes to matters of hospitality, we do all our own work: the shopping, the cooking, the serving, the cleanup. For large parties, we may occasionally hire a couple of students from Columbia University to tend bar and scrub glasses, but that is the fullest extent of our extravagance.

I tell myself that I like it that way, and I think it's the truth. I would, of course, be perfectly happy if I never had to wash another fork again, but doing the dishes is a price I happily pay to maintain full and absolute control. Nothing could induce me to entrust my guests to a mercenary. A caterer may be and probably is the better cook; he will surely go to more trouble than I do to present his fare elegantly; he almost certainly has a more refined appreciation of wine and how to select it; he may smile more than I do over the course of an evening, and will speak more pleasingly and offer more subtle flattery to my guests. But he is not the host – he is not me – and he can never hope to give the guests what they really want or to secure for the host the less tangible rewards of hospitality. Most important, being greedy of praise, I couldn't possibly tolerate having to share it.

The catered dinner party is theater in a language I do not speak. It violates almost every rule of hospitality. I find no magic, no transcendence, no vision of utopia, no intimacy there. This is not because there is something intrinsically inferior about a catered dinner, but because such an affair requires host and guest alike to surrender an essential element of their humanity. Hospitality is a song of himself that the host sings to his guests. It is also communication, a reciprocal conversation of the deepest intimacy. You could argue that having an event catered gives the host more freedom and focus for that conversation. I say it is all of a piece; anyone can relax when someone else is doing all the work. It is the ability to see to everything personally and still show your guests how pleasant and honorable it is to serve them that communicates your concern for them. How can you have this conversation when you are speaking through a spokesperson, your caterer? For whom does the caterer speak? Is he advertising your generosity or his own talents? When Colin Cowie caters a wedding, who is the star? At a catered event, the host may be singing a beautiful song, but his face is veiled and you suspect that he is lip-synching.

This is what weddings are all about: the creation of a language that avoids affective human intercourse and seeks to project an abstracted idea about the host – power, status, wealth, influence, patronage – rather than the reality of the host himself. The proof of this, in my experience, is that the only people who ever truly enjoy a wedding are those intimately connected to the newlyweds' families, who can override the disembodiment of the emotional experience. The rest of us have to submit to it and content ourselves with poached salmon and oldies dance tunes.

What choice does the host have, you might ask, if he wishes to invite two hundred people to his daughter's wedding? He can't very well cook for them, can he? To which I can only respond: Why does he need to invite two hundred people when everyone he loves in this world can fit in one medium-size room? For whom is the wedding supposed to be if not for them? I know this is an unfair question based on unrealistic assumptions, but it still bears asking. After all, weddings have been catered for thousands of years, consistently with the same end in mind. I understand perfectly well that your typical wedding has never been an intimate family affair on a par with, say, Thanksgiving or a *bris*, but that is precisely my point – a wedding is always about something else. If a father of the bride finds it necessary to invite his clients or business associates, he must be honest with himself and acknowledge that he is exploiting the happiest day of his child's life to project an exaggerated and sanitized message of his own social standing.

That is why the hospitality of a powerful person – a politician, say, or a wealthy patron, as we have seen in earlier chapters – is always fraught with anxiety and confusion for the guest. Like yours and mine, his hospitality is a powerful form of self-expression; unlike yours and mine, his is deliberately couched in the idiom of remove. You know that he has chosen this language to conceal at least as much as he reveals about himself; what you cannot hope to know, because he does not want you to know, is precisely what it is he is concealing. This perversion of all that is potentially fine and ennobling in the conversation of souls is at the very heart of his power over you – the host as Grand Inquisitor. No one understands this duplicity of the potentate better than his caterer.

Olivier de La Marche was born to serve. His family, of the minor nobility of Bresse, had been in the service of the dukes of Burgundy since the thirteenth century. His grandfather had served with distinction in the household of Philip the Bold, the first Valois duke of Burgundy. His aunt had served as lady-in-waiting to Duchess Marguerite, Philip's wife. His uncle had served as equerry and cupbearer to Philip's son, John the Fearless. His father had served as warden of the forest of Burgundy and as counselor and chamberlain to John's son, Philip the Good, the third Valois duke. In 1439, Olivier's patron presented him to the ducal court, where the fourteen-year-old boy was taken into service as a page.

It is safe to say that the La Marche family owed everything to the house of Burgundy, and that they knew it. They reciprocated with a blind loyalty that bordered on cultish devotion. Such fidelity was supposed to be the norm in feudal society, but in the case of the La Marches it was all the more deferential by virtue of their acute awareness of the honor and glory of living in the golden age of Burgundy. Anyone who was ever involved in the households of the four Valois dukes could not help but recognize that it was the grandest court in Europe, not excluding the royal establishments in Paris, London, and Madrid or the imperial court in Vienna. To actually live among and serve the dukes of Burgundy was to experience the very acme of the knightly tradition and medieval pageantry. The wealth, the color, the pomp, and the glory would have dazzled a mind far more independent, creative, and skeptical than young Olivier's; as it was, the young man threw himself into unquestioning, slavish service with tireless zeal and gratitude.

The Valois family had been dukes since 1363, when King John II of France had given the dukedom to his son, Philip the Bold. The power struggle that began then between the two Valois branches, Burgundy and Orléans, grew nastier and fiercer with every succeeding generation, fueled by the Hundred Years War. Burgundy slowly began to swallow up its neighbors: Artois, Flanders, Franche-Comté, the Netherlands, the Ardennes, Hainaut, Brabant, and Luxembourg all became Burgundian territories. In 1407, John the Fearless ordered the assassination of Louis, duc d'Orléans, the king's brother. The Orléans retaliated in kind against John twelve years later; his son Philip the Good recognized Henry VI of England as his suzerain and pursued the war against France. A peace treaty was signed in 1435 that made further territorial concessions to Burgundy. By 1450, the house of Burgundy had courts in Dijon, Brussels, and Bruges and controlled territories encompassing most of the modern Netherlands, Belgium, Luxembourg, and northern and eastern France. The Burgundian state stretched nearly to Lyon and its western border came within fifty miles of Paris.

It was around this time that Olivier de La Marche, recently promoted to pantler-squire, left the service of Philip the Good to become secretary to the duke's son, Charles, count of Charolais. It must have seemed like a good move at the time. It was true that Olivier had prospered under Philip, a fine man, proud, beloved, and lusty, whom Olivier would later describe as more like "a chivalrous gentleman, performing bold and valiant deeds," than a great prince. If he were perhaps given to unbridled fits of rage, he was also praised for his "quality of moderation" and ability to forgive and forget. If he was associated with certain unpleasant moments, such as the sale of Joan of Arc to the English for ten thousand gold crowns, he was also the founder of the Low Countries and a true Frenchman who regretted his entire life not having fought for his country at Agincourt. Philip was a credit to his family, Burgundy, and chivalry.

But he had been duke for some thirty years, while young Charles, still in his teens, represented the future. Olivier was ambitious not just for himself but also for the house in which he served, and Charles already seemed destined to carry the momentum of Burgundy's century to its natural culmination: the establishment of an independent kingdom. As a boy, he had stayed up late into the night reading the old stories of Lancelot and Gawain, Hannibal and Caesar, delighting most especially in the exploits of Alexander the Great, who, like him, was a son of a Philip. Charles was the first of his line to speak fluent Flemish and English. He was the very embodiment of knighthood, a fine jouster, fighter, hunter, and sportsman. "He was hot, active, and impetuous: as a child he was very eager to have his own way," says La Marche. Most unusually for the time, he had been breast-fed by his mother, Isabella of Portugal, whose suspicious nature he seems to have inherited. Was he perhaps aloof, austere, friendless, of hasty temper, impetuous, vindictive? Did he lack serenity and collegiality? Did his swarthy complexion, icy blue eyes, prim mouth, and protruding jaw reveal a certain latent barbarism? Never mind – he was a great lord and Olivier was his man to the end. "It may be said hereafter," he would later write, "that I praise him highly in my writings because he was my master. To that, I respond that I am telling the truth and that I knew him to be thus. Any vices that he may have had were never apparent to me." Philip may have been the Good, but Charles was the Bold.

Philip lived on, while Charles and Olivier chaffed. There was a job to do, and the moment of truth seemed tantalizingly close at hand, but the aging Philip fell just short of the energy and ruthlessness needed to see it through. Several Burgundian kingdoms had thrived since the fall of Rome; the destruction of the first is the subject of the *Nibelungenlied*; the kingdom of Lotharingia had extended from the North Sea to the Mediterranean. It could do so again, and soon. The family was strong enough; the court already richer and more splendid than any royal court; the glories of Burgundian arms, architecture, arts, and letters were the envy of Europe; and almost all of the necessary territories were in place. All that was needed was the acquisition of Alsace, Lorraine, and Provence, and Charles could be king, even if Philip would not. Lotharingia could rise again, but it would have to be on the ruins of France. As Charles himself put it, he loved France so much that he would have liked her to have six kings instead of one. Philippe de Commynes, who knew Charles intimately, limned his ambition more grimly: "Even the half of Europe would not have satisfied him."

In 1465, the great princes of France – Burgundy, Brittany, Normandy, Bourbon, and Berry – waged the War of the Public Good against King Louis XI, and the moment seemed at hand. One decisive military campaign would topple the king and dismember France for good. Charles led the princes at the battle of Montlhéry, with Olivier de La Marche at his side. When Charles broke one wing of the royal army and sent it into panicked flight, all seemed lost for the king. But instead of consolidating his strength, Charles ignored all the advice of his commanders in order to pursue the fleeing Frenchmen. By the time he returned to the battlefield, only to find the rest of Louis's army intact, his men were exhausted from the chase. The battle was fought to an inconclusive standstill, but Paris and the king survived. Lotharingia would have to wait. Olivier must have experienced certain nagging doubts about his suzerain's fitness to command, but the knighthood he received on the battlefield would have made them easy to suppress.

The year 1467 finally brought the long-awaited death of Philip the Good and the accession of Charles the Bold as fourth Valois duke of Burgundy. His personal inheritance, according to La Marche, was "four hundred thousand crowns of gold cash, seventy-two thousand marks of silver plate, without counting rich tapestries, rings, gold dishes garnished with precious stones, a large and well-equipped library, and rich furniture." He wasted not one moment, dispatching Olivier de La Marche on a secret mission to England forthwith. La Marche soon returned with Edward IV's promise of his sister, Margaret of York, in marriage to the new duke. The news of the betrothal rang out like a thunderclap across western Europe.

Charles was a direct descendant of John of Gaunt, the first Plantagenet duke of Lancaster. Thus, for him to marry Margaret – a Yorkist, an enemy of France, and sister of the king who had deposed the Lancastrian Henry VI – could only mean one thing: a reversal of Burgundian foreign policy. This marriage was, in essence, Charles's notification to Louis XI of his intention to resume the Hundred Years War. To France, facing the triple threat of an Anglo-Burgundian-Germanic alliance, the wedding bells would have sounded an awful lot like a death knell. And Olivier de La Marche was in charge of organizing the festivities.

To call the wedding of Charles the Bold to Margaret of York "the marriage of the century," as many historians have done, is almost an understatement. This marriage had the potential to alter the entire makeup of Western Europe. And since Western Europe was only decades away from launching the greatest era of exploration, colonization, and international trade the world has ever known, it is not too much of a stretch to say that this wedding held all world history in the balance. Try to imagine the history of North America without France or the history of Africa and Southeast Asia without the Netherlands. Now try to imagine that you are Olivier de La Marche, responsible for conveying the message of Charles's ambitions via the medium of one single event, one momentous, obliterating, omniphagous act of hospitality. Every wedding sends a message. How would you advise the caterer if yours was that you were intent on conquering the world? What would Colin Cowie do?

Of course, La Marche had been waiting his whole life for this opportunity. He had had a dress rehearsal in 1454, when he had helped organize the Feast of the Pheasant to mobilize a new crusade against the Turks, who had finally taken Constantinople the year before. The crusade came to naught, but the feast had been a spectacular success. Still, it was nothing compared to this wedding, which was going to be nothing less than the apotheosis of Charles, Burgundy, and the ideals of medieval knighthood.

Edward IV gave his sister a dowry of two hundred thousand pounds and sent her across the Channel with a large flotilla and a trousseau that included £1,000 worth of silks; £160 in gold, silver, and gilt dishes; and £100 of bedding, cushions, and carpets. She landed in Sluis on June 25, 1468, wearing a wedding coronet of gold trimmed with pearls, precious stones, enameled white roses, and a diamond cross over her long blond hair – every inch the medieval princess. The streets of Sluis were carpeted in her honor. She was introduced to her fiancé by the Bishop of Salisbury, whom protocol required to ascertain that she was willing to go through with the wedding. It was for that reason and no other, she responded, that she had been sent by her brother, the king of England, and what the king had commanded, she was ready to undertake and accomplish. The next week, she sailed upriver with her retinue for the private wedding ceremony in Damme. Then, borne in a gilded litter and wearing a gown of white cloth of gold, she was accompanied by the greatest peers of the realm in thirteen white hackneys draped with crimson cloth of gold to the Gate of Saint Croix in Bruges, where the wedding festivities were ready to begin.

Bruges in the fifteenth century was one of the wealthiest cities of northern Europe, a bustling mercantile center home to bankers, jewelers, goldsmiths, and cloth merchants. Now it had the eyes of a continent upon it. A vast press of Flemish nobility met Margaret at the gate, and she was led by four official processions through streets garlanded with flowers and hung with carpets and tapestries. The horses were draped in gold cloth. The members of the processions wore robes of black damask and doublets of crimson satin; embroidered gowns of black satin; black and violet brocade and pourpoints – all paid for by the duke at a cost of some forty thousand francs. Ten tableaux vivants – representing, among other things, God ushering Adam and Eve into the Garden of Eden, and Cleopatra's marriage to Alexander [sic] – were set up at strategic points along the route. At last, the bride arrived at the ducal palace, where a forty-foot tower, teeming with monkeys, wolves, and bears, and a golden pelican perched on an artificial tree, spurting sweet hippocras from its breast, had been erected in the courtyard.

An enormous wooden banquet hall, some 140 by 70 feet, had also been raised there, boasting two upper galleries, glass windows with gilded shutters, and mirrored chandeliers in the form of castles. The ceilings were draped in blue and white wool, the walls in tapestries of silk, wool, and gold and silver thread, depicting the arms of Burgundy and the story of Jason and the Golden Fleece. As the historian Christine Weightman points out, even one set of such tapestries might cost the equivalent of the total annual income of a noble landowner. Three enormous buffet tables groaned under the weight of crystal, gold, silver, and copper plate, encrusted with precious gems. Three hundred men labored in the kitchen, eighty in the *saucerie*, sixty in the wine room, sixty in the bakery, and fifteen in the pantry to prepare the banquet.

La Marche, typical of medieval chroniclers, does not include a menu in his description of the banquet, but it is not hard to imagine. At the Feast of the Pheasant, each course consisted of forty-eight dishes; the wedding banquet certainly had no fewer. In his *Le Viandier*, Guillaume Tirel, chief cook to Charles VI of France, had set down a wealth of recipes that were most representative of the diversity of the medieval aristocratic table, and we can assume that many of these dishes were served at Charles the Bold's wedding. The boiled meats would have included beef, pork, mutton, venison, boar, and capon, served with sauces of green garlic; white garlic; parsley, sage, and hyssop; mustard; sharp pepper; or cameline, a favorite sauce composed of ginger, cinnamon, cloves, grains of paradise, mace, and pickled pepper and thickened with bread. The roasts, often served with verjuice, would have included pork, tripe, mutton, kid, goslings, pigeons, larks, quail, thrush, plovers, woodcock, partridge, turtle doves, swan, peacock, pheasant, stork, heron, bustards, bitterns, cormorant, spoonbills, and teal. There would have been a great deal of soup, such as cuminade of fish, bright green brewet of eels, gravy of Loach, chaudumel of pike, oyster stew, mustard sops, egg stew, and brewet of stag testicles. Among the more exotic dishes there may have been faulxgrenon (chopped livers and gizzards with bacon grease, ginger, cinnamon, cloves, grains of paradise, and egg yolk), pettitoes (feet, livers, and gizzards), frumenty (grains of wheat, boiled and mashed with milk, saffron, and egg yolk), fried milk, Spanish farts (boiled egg whites stuffed with meatballs and glazed with batter), and swans redressed in their skin. The predominant seasonings were ginger, cardamom, cinnamon, cloves, grain of paradise, long pepper, aspic, round pepper, cassia buds, saffron, nutmeg, bay leaf, galingale, mace, laurel, cumin, sugar, almonds, garlic, onions, and shallots.

Perhaps the most unusual dish on the medieval menu was the cockentrice. You start with a piglet and a capon, each of which is neatly bisected. The front part of the piglet is then sewn on to the back end of the capon, and the front part of the capon to the back end of the piglet. These two creatures are then stuffed with forcemeat, roasted on a spit, and repeatedly glazed with saffron, egg yolk, and powdered ginger until they appear to be gilded with gold leaf. There was something about these perverse hybrids that appealed to the medieval sense of awe and mystery, like the ubiquitous dragons, griffins, and unicorns of heraldry. There was also something strangely ambiguous and subversive about them in an age when everything had its divinely ordained place and identity that no human interference could disrupt. To be confused about who or what you were in feudal society was to be nothing at all.

But food was hardly the central element of a medieval banquet. Dinner was theater, replete with music, religious pageants, dancing, plays and poetry on historic themes, acrobats, dwarves, ogres, giants, wild animals, elaborate sculptures, and mechanical wonders known as *entremets*. The Feast of the Pheasant had featured a twenty-eight-piece orchestra in an enormous pie crust. The wedding banquet, of course, was no less dramatic. The duke wore a robe woven with gold and encrusted with diamonds, pearls, and enormous jewels. The courses were served in thirty gold and azure ships, fully rigged, each one bearing the arms of one of Charles's seignories, including five duchies and fourteen counties. Harts carried baskets of fruit to the guests. A silk-clad unicorn entered, ridden by a leopard bearing the arms of England and a daisy (*marguerite*) in honor of the bride. Next came a gilded lion, ridden by Madame de Beaugrand, Lady Mary's dwarf. The lion sang a song, then kneeled in homage before the new duchess. It was followed by a dromedary ridden by a wild man, who threw brightly painted birds among the guests. Later, there were monsters and griffons and a staging of the deeds of Hercules and the marriage of Clovis.

The festivities lasted ten days, with banquets and jousting in the marketplace on each. Watching it all from the sidelines, Olivier de La Marche must have been well pleased. In the households of the dukes, he had been proud to serve as page, equerry, pantler, master carver, maître d'hotel, ambassador, warrior, poet, chronicler, and caterer, but he had to know that this was his true moment of glory. At the Feast of the Pheasant, some fourteen years earlier, he had paused briefly to condemn the extravagance of the hospitality. "I considered the whole thing outrageous and without any justification." There was no such outrage now. A wiser and more cynical man, perhaps, schooled in Charles's ruthless version of realpolitik, he knew full well that the expense was entirely justified. "Great and honorable achievements deserve a lasting renown and perpetual remembrance." In the short term, with a royal dynasty to establish, and in the long term, with the eternal splendor of Burgundy to glorify, Olivier had helped to ensure that the hospitality of Charles the Bold would, indeed, be remembered forever. And because Olivier's entire identity was invested in service, Charles's glory was his glory.

What he could not know was that the wedding would be remembered not as the glorious dawn of a new era, but as a swan song, the spectacular final act of a dying star in supernova.

You might even call it the last great hurrah of the Middle Ages themselves. Within nine years – despite maneuvering Louis XI into a brilliant trap that resulted in unprecedented concessions; despite luring Edward IV into an invasion of France; despite putting together a seemingly invincible international alliance – Charles had squandered all of Burgundy's strength, talent, and goodwill. In 1476, he was twice decisively defeated by the Swiss, at Grandson and Morat. His mental health deteriorating, he took to drinking and plotting irrational and unrealistic revenge. "His ears were blocked, and his mind disordered," wrote Philippe de Commynes. In 1477, having undertaken an ill-advised siege of Nancy, the capital of Lorraine, he was killed in the press, his naked and mutilated body found in a muddy pond a few days later. The Burgundian state was dismantled and portioned off to France and the Empire. Burgundy was now a mere "province" and would never rise again.

Olivier stuck it out with Charles to the bitter end, unable to envision any alternative to his increasingly thankless service. He had plenty of opportunity and cause to defect, and several generous offers from Louis, but unlike Commynes – who had crossed over in 1472, to his great moral and financial benefit – he passed them all up. Without Burgundy, he was nothing. True, Charles rewarded his loyalty by appointing him treasurer of Guelders, but this can have been of scant comfort. The nadir of his service must have been when, desperate and irrational, Charles ordered him in 1476 to kidnap Yolande, Louis XI's sister and duchess of Savoy. He carried out his orders, but ambivalently and in great disgust. Kidnapping noble ladies was not in the job description of a faithful knight. Had ever a loyal subject been served up as such a cockentrice? These were his thanks for catering the wedding of the century? He was taken prisoner at Nancy and ransomed for four thousand écus. Upon his release, he returned to Flanders, where he went into service as premier maître d'hôtel to Mary, Charles's daughter, now married to the Habsburg Archduke Maximilian. He was appointed tutor to their son, Philip the Handsome, and set about writing mediocre poetry (including an allegorical poem in praise of Charles) and a detailed account, commissioned by Edward IV, of the management of Charles the Bold's household. His motto, appended to all his writings, was *Tant a souffert La Marche* – roughly, "The long-suffering La Marche." In his memoirs, a hundred of the 150 pages that La Marche devotes to the reign of Charles the Bold are spent describing the wedding.

Hitler, Louis XIV, and Charles the Bold were all perfectly well aware that hospitality in the service of ideology is no hospitality at all. Like poetry, genuine hospitality cannot work unless it is direct and immediate, an unmediated conversation. Otherwise, it becomes something else – propaganda, advertising, sublimated desire. Like poetry, it must be honest, even if it is merely conveying an honest cry for praise, recognition, or comfort. A failure of honesty fatally compromises hospitality and host alike.

There was surely a moment when Olivier de La Marche felt as if he were the host at Charles's wedding. It is easy to imagine him standing at the sidelines in his black damask and crimson doublet, responding in subdued and false modesty to the compliments, yet sensing himself the dark star around which it all revolved. This, surely, was ample payment for a life of subservience. And just as surely, Charles must have felt – as many men do at their own weddings – that he was a guest, a bystander to his own glory. It is sad – at least, it is sorry – to think of these two deluded men, both spinning away into nothingness in their moment of greatest pride and arrogance. They were both victims of their own dishonesty, cockentrices hybridized by their devotion to an abstraction, and both were destroyed by it. In this, hospitality betrayed is like a wronged goddess and will not rest until she has exacted her revenge.

CHAPTER VI

GERMANS!

A great many things keep happening, some of them good, some of them bad. The inhabitants of different countries keep quarrelling fiercely with each other and kings go on losing their tempers in the most furious way.
Gregory of Tours, *History of the Franks*

When Jesus Christ was still a little boy preaching to the rabbis, the Consul Varus Quintilius left Rome on a quixotic mission. He crossed the empire's northern border and entered the heart of Germany "as though he were going among a people enjoying the blessings of peace," despite all evidence to the contrary. Somehow, the consul had convinced himself that the Germans, "who could not be subdued by the sword, could be soothed by the law." The German prince Arminius destroyed his army and sent his head back to Rome on a platter. It was a pattern with which the Romans were to become increasingly familiar.

Rome had known nothing about the Germans in the second century B.C. and only gained its first real sense of them in Julius Caesar's northern campaigns late in the first. One hundred years later, the empire was surrounded. Scandinavia was Germanic; the lands of modern Germany swarmed with Franks, Suebi, Chatti, Saxons, and myriad smaller tribes and confederacies; a vast eastward migration swept Germanic Goths, Vandals, Burgundians, and Langobards onto the plains of eastern Europe and

Scythia, whence they gradually began their westward drive against the far eastern frontiers of the empire.

The Rhine was the border between Germany and Gaul, as it is today. To the hapless Gauls, softened by generations of wine-drinking, toga-wearing, villa-living, and other Roman necessities, the river offered scant protection from the *feri* – the wild animals – on the other side. "Little by little they have grown accustomed to defeat," Julius Caesar says of the Gauls, "and after being conquered in many battles they do not even compare themselves in point of valour with the Germans." The Gauls were so terrified by the Germans that they were "unable even to endure their look and the keenness of their eyes." Gaul was like a pampered teenage girl, Rome's beloved eldest, blushing and squirming under the hardened gaze of a merciless Lothario. He would have her, she knew, the moment papa's back was turned.

These Germans really were different in every way. They were illiterate and proud of it. They worshipped only what they could see: the sun, the moon, water, fire. They hated cities, knew nothing of stonemasonry, and lived in villages of widely scattered huts. Even in the coldest weather, they wore nothing but cloaks or skins fastened with a thorn, training themselves to hardship; only the most distinguished wore underwear. The German prince Ariovistus boasted of his "invincible Germans highly trained in arms, who in a period of fourteen years had never been beneath a roof." They ate boiled meat and curdled milk and drank only beer, fearing that wine would make them "soft and womanish." They slept late and spent their lives hunting, fighting, and getting drunk. "To make day and night run into one in drinking is a reproach to no man," claimed Tacitus. "Brawls are frequent, naturally, among heavy drinkers: they are seldom settled with abuse, more often with wounds and bloodshed." There was no criminal law but that of vendetta and *wergeld* – blood price –

whereby most any crime, including murder, could be atoned for by paying a fixed number of cattle and sheep, "and the whole family thereby receives satisfaction." At the same time, young men were strongly encouraged to abstain from sex, which was thought to deplete their youthful vigor, and highly admired for their chastity.

The Germans also enjoyed freedoms that even the most repressed Roman could not help but envy, in a horror-stricken kind of way. Their "freedom of life – for from boyhood up they are not schooled in a sense of duty or discipline, and do nothing whatever against their wish – nurses their strength and makes men of immense bodily stature." They would endure no kings, but ruled themselves by assemblies and elected chieftains and warlords. They owned no land privately, but every year were assigned new plots to cultivate so as to prevent covetousness, avert the rise of economic disparities, and discourage attachment to any particular farmstead, which it was feared would sap the warrior spirit. They bathed in rivers.

In brief, short of the Huns, the Germans were as unlike Latins as it was possible to be. It was a cultural divide that only the most optimistic among us would claim to be reconciled today.

The fall of the Roman Empire is too complex and grand a subject to be addressed here. To keep it simple, over the course of several centuries it was gradually overrun, partially by Asians, mostly by Germans. In the year 410, the Visigoth Alaric, having plundered, destroyed, and slaughtered his way through Italy, besieged Rome, driving it to the brink of starvation, but was unable to take it by force. Alaric may have been a pagan barbarian, but he knew his Romans. He chose three hundred of the most attractive teenage boys in his army and gave them to the patricians of Rome as a peace offering. While Alaric made show of lifting the siege, the boys set about making themselves indispensable to their doting new masters. Then one day, when the patricians were relaxing and napping after their lunch – as their descendants continue to do to this day – on a predetermined signal the young Visigoths stole away, converged on the Salarian gate, slew the guards, and opened the city to the invader. Rome, it seems, fell not to the Visigoths but to the seductions of a heavy *pranzo*. When told of the destruction of Rome, the Emperor Honorius, safe behind the ramparts of Ravenna, was greatly relieved to learn that it was Roma the city, and not his prize rooster Roma, that had died.

Rome did not officially collapse until 476, but by then its entire western empire was safely in the hands of Germans. The Ostrogoths and Lombards held Italy, the Visigoths Spain, and the Vandals Libya. Gaul was chiefly occupied by Franks in the north, Burgundians in the east, and Goths in the south. Angles, Saxons, and Jutes were crushing the Romanized Celts of Britain, many of whom sought refuge in northwestern Gaul, creating Brittany, which was subsequently crushed by the Franks. The process of Christianizing western Europe had to start all over again.

There is good reason why this age of German ascendancy is known as the Dark Ages. I mentioned that the Germans were illiterate; it took them centuries to begin setting down their own history in writing. In the meantime, literacy was preserved by the few surviving literate Christian clerics, who tended (especially in Gaul) to descend from the conquered peoples and did not always put the gentlest spin on the activities of their overlords. Then, too, because they had no tradition of centralized inherited power, the Germans took far too long to stop squabbling among themselves over what was essentially booty. The few surviving histories of the era are basically nothing more than the annals of centuries of ceaseless warfare, piracy, intrigue, martyrdom, misrule, fratricide, and natural disaster. "To this day," Gregory of Tours wrote in the preface to his *History of the Franks*, "one is still amazed and astonished at the disasters which befell these people."

What is astonishing is how long these Germans in Gaul and Britain remained truly German, with all that implies. In Britain, it is true, they wiped out, enslaved, and exiled the native peoples and thus left no indigenous culture into which they might be absorbed. Indeed, they used the same word to indicate "foreigner" and "slave" – *wealh* – which came to mean native Briton and eventually evolved into "Welsh." For many centuries they clung to the system of the old country, establishing feuding kingdoms, loosely based on ancient tribal divisions, that endured into the tenth century. By that time they were calling themselves *Angelcynn* and their language *Englisc*, but even in the tenth century Athelstan was still referring to himself as "King of the Anglo-Saxons." Had it not been for the Norman invasion, the English today would be as Germanic as the Austrians or the Dutch.

In Gaul, the story played out a little differently. There was no question of the Franks' wiping out the natives, who were more docile than the Britons and too useful as chattel. Instead, the Franks superimposed their nobility onto the old Roman villa system of farming estates and acted as a separate society of overlords. Understandably, the modern French pronounce the names of their early Germanic kings – Dagobert, Clovis, Chilperic, Guntram – to make them sound comfortably familiar, cuddly enough for French schoolchildren, but they were as German as they come. Charlemagne was really Karl der Grosse and built his capital in Aachen. Anyone doubting the genuine Germanness of the great French hero need only consider the names of his daughters – Hruodrud, Bertha, Gisela, Theoderada, Hiltrud, Ruodhaid, and Adaltrud. Even his most French-sounding son Louis the Pious was, in reality, named Hludowic. When Charlemagne renamed the months, it was not as *janvier*, *février, mars, avril,* and so on, but as *Wintarmanoth, Hornung, Lentzinmanoth,* and *Ostarmanoth.* And this was after the Franks had been in Gaul so long – more than five centuries – that some were beginning to call their country Francia. Meanwhile, the debased vernacular Latin of the Gauls was evolving very nicely into Old French, almost entirely unadulterated by German. It is a measure of how aloof the Frankish rulers maintained themselves from their subjects, century after century, that there are barely a thousand words of German origin in modern French.

How did the Germans spend this lengthy idyll in Gaul, as close to Hitler's dream of pan-European hegemony as they were ever to get? Did they use this time to improve themselves, to evolve as a people, to cultivate the arts and letters, manners and hospitality, to embue themselves with the spirit of their newfound Christianity? Did they exalt the platform of empire to bring peace, prosperity, and a unifying culture to those they had conquered, as the Romans had done? To carry the message of Germanic democracy, freedoms, and civil rights to their benighted provinces? Well, not exactly.

They pretty much remained just as Caesar, Tacitus, and Velleius Paterculus had described them: illiterate, seminomadic, hard-drinking brawlers with no interest in good food, nice clothes, discipline, or peace and quiet. The Greeks of Byzantium had a saying: "Have the Frank for your friend, but not for your neighbor." They seemed to know what they were talking about.

As a result of all this, the few remaining records of that period offer precious little documentation for the historian of hospitality. In some ways, this is actually the anti-hospitality chapter, concerned with what the world looks like in the absence of hospitality. There is practically no record of domestic life, domestic architecture, food culture, or the mores of hospitality from the Dark Ages. Domesticity does not seem to have existed as a virtue, at least not among the recorders of history and their circles. This may be due to the fact that, what with marauding German warriors everywhere, the constant threat of famine and plague, the lack of safe sanctuary, even in churches, and the decay of the Roman road system, there was little traveling done and not much use for a culture of hospitality. Gone were the sumptuous villas; gone the well-heeled domestic slaves; gone the ancient vineyards; gone the well-worn trade routes bringing luxury commodities from throughout Europe, Asia, and Africa to elegant centers of commerce and learning; gone the straight paved roads patrolled by officers of the peace; gone the rule of encoded law; long gone any memory of Pax Romana. It may also be that, as Gregory noted, there was so much going on and so few people capable of writing it all down that those who could had to concentrate on affairs of state and church. But a careful study of the primary sources inevitably leads one back again and again to another conclusion: they were all too busy drinking and fighting to entertain.

While it may be true that serving drinks to one's friends is a form of hospitality, the Germanic conquest of Gaul was no cocktail party. What Tacitus had said about the Germans in the first century – "They banish hunger without great preparation or appetizing sauces, but there is not the same temperance in facing thirst" – still held true in the eighth. They really had no interest in food culture. Charlemagne's physician thought him shockingly decadent for preferring roast meat over boiled. Germanic poets and annalists never wrote about food; whenever they did refer to banqueting and the treatment of guests, it was to emphasize the drinking, which was central and symbolic to their civic decision-making process. The historian Hugh Magennis notes that, in *Beowulf*, warriors sit at an "ale-bench" or a "mead-bench," while Heorot is referred to variously as a "mead-hall," a "beer-hall," and a "wine-hall," but never as a place to eat, despite the fact that plenty of eating must have gone on there. Even in the Anglo-Saxon Bible, the Latin *convivium* (feast) is usually translated as *gebeorscipe* – "beer fest" – as in "Queen Esther invited King Xerxes to a beer fest."

Chieftains owed any power they might have to their ability to attract followers, who were bound to them by a simple quid pro quo: so long as the chieftain could feed them, supply them with weapons, and provide continuous opportunities to freeboot, his "companions" remained prepared to die for him. Neither kinship, family loyalty, nor tribal affiliation played much part in this relationship. A warrior was perfectly lost without a lord, but so long as he was able to find a new one who was willing to assume responsibility for him (and for any debts he might have incurred as a result of having committed crimes, including murder, that were forgivable through the payment of a fine), he was free to go where and with whom he wished. Beowulf himself tersely summarizes the nature of his relationship to his chief: "I repaid him in battle for the treasures which he gave me." It was as simple as that. The poem itself is merely an account of a freelance assignment, a percentage of the profits of which go to the contractor.

Drinking played a major role in cementing the bonds of this association. As Tacitus points out, drunken banquets were the accepted venue for any serious negotiation, including "the mutual reconciliation of enemies, the forming of family alliances, the appointment of chiefs, the question even of war or peace." When Beowulf arrives in Denmark, he finds Hrothgar and his Danes greatly demoralized by Grendel's gruesome predations. Night after night, the monster raids Heorot and carries off up to thirty hapless warriors to his lair; and yet, night after night, the king entertains his company, slips away with his queen to a secluded bower in the royal compound, and leaves his men to settle in the mead hall for the night, "a company of the best asleep from their feasting, insensible to pain and human sorrow." Why? Hasn't anyone ever asked themselves why these valiant defenders of the realm sleep night after night in the one place in all Scandinavia where they can be sure their invincible foe – a "God-cursed brute," a "shadow-stalker," a "captain of evil" – will seek them out in their most vulnerable condition? Even if we allow that there were few Solomons among these sixth-century pagan thugs, how are we to understand the Danes' obdurate self-destructive compulsion?

In a word, Hrothgar keeps the boys in line by keeping them drunk. "Time and again, when the goblets passed and seasoned fighters got flushed with beer they would pledge themselves to protect Heorot and wait for Grendel with whetted swords." But they didn't wait; they passed out every time, and "When dawn broke and day crept in over each empty, blood-spattered bench, the floor of the mead-hall where they had feasted would be slick with slaughter." Hrothgar is described as humiliated, bewildered, and numb with grief, but this is a little hard to swallow, since the bower in which he sleeps is explicitly described as enjoying divine protection. In other words, every night this brave king fills the bellies of these simple boys – under the circumstances, "simple" must be taken as a charitable characterization – with free beer and boiled game and their ears with cheap flattery, then slinks off to his guaranteed safe haven, but not before ensuring that they have pledged their lives to defeating a creature they will be too drunk to rise and challenge.

A number of early historians related as fact that the Germans first arrived in Britain in the mid-fifth century at the invitation of the British – softened by centuries of Roman occupation and unable to defend themselves since the withdrawal of the legions in 410 – to fight as mercenaries against the wild Scots and Picts.

Nennius relates how the British King Vortigern, unable to feed and pay them, asks the Germans to leave. Instead, their leader Hengist imports more soldiers, along with his beautiful teenage daughter. Hengist holds a celebration banquet for Vortigern, who gets drunk and falls in love with the girl, just as Hengist had planned. Hengist demands Kent in return for the girl, and thus the Germans establish their first foothold in Britain. It doesn't really matter that this is almost certainly a tall tale – everyone of Nennius' time knew that this was the way the Germans did things.

In varying degrees of sincerity, the Anglo-Saxons and the Franks received Christianity in the sixth and seventh centuries, which allowed them to look down upon their pagan kinsmen in the old country but otherwise seems to have had little effect on their weltanschauung. The truth is, they probably did not know what they were getting themselves into and imagined that they were merely trading in a bunch of minor woodland gods for one essentially similar but more powerful. It's likely that many converts didn't even bother abandoning the old gods but merely added the new one to their pantheon. Many of the earliest churches were simply consecrated pagan temples with the idols removed. Very little Christian teaching was offered to the early converts. All that was required of a pagan wishing to convert was to swear a simple oath:

> Q: Forsachistu diobolae? (Do you forsake the Devil?)
> A: Ec forsacho diobolae. (I forsake the Devil.)
> Q: End alum diobolgeldae? (And all devil-worship?)
> A: End ec forsacho alum diobolgeldae (. . .)
> Q: Gelobistu in got alamehtigan fadær? (Do you believe in God the Father Almighty?)
> A: Ec gelobo etc. (I believe, etc.)

Q: Gelobistu in crist godes suno? (Do you believe in Christ, God's son?)
A: Ec gelobo etc.
Q: Gelobistu in halogan gast? (Do you believe in the holy ghost?)
A: Ec gelobo etc.

The sacrament of baptism was just as unlikely to inculcate an understanding of God's infinite mercy, the mysteries of the Trinity, or any other abstraction that was held to distinguish the new religion from the old. Consider the perfectly reasonable irritation of the pagan Viking marauder on being required to wear a baptismal robe:

> I have gone through this washing business here twenty times already, and I have been dressed in excellent clothes of perfect whiteness; but a sack like this is more fit for clodhoppers than for soldiers. If I were not afraid of my nakedness, for you have taken away my own clothes and have given me no new ones, I would soon leave your wrap and your Christ as well.

Nor did the behavior of the clergy offer the Germans any reason to think that converting to Christianity required some sort of conversion to civility, sobriety, or mercy. Contemporary accounts positively stagger under the weight of drunken, violent clerics. Gregory of Tours offers us a few saintly lives, but virtually every page of his history shows clergymen behaving badly. A newly appointed bishop, "loaded with food, drenched with liquor and buried in wine, . . . failed to go to the evening service." "Once he had taken possession of his bishopric, Cautinus began to behave so badly that he was soon loathed by everybody. He began to drink heavily. He was so often so completely fuddled with wine that it would take four men to carry him from the table." In battle, Bishops Salonius and Sagittarius "armed themselves like laymen and killed many men with their own hands. They engaged in a quarrel with their own congregations and beat quite a few of them with wooden clubs." "There lived in the town of Le Mans a certain priest, who was fond of fine living and who was always having affairs." "After his consecration as Bishop he took to drink." The priest Eufrasius "would ply the Franks with drink, but he very rarely gave refreshment to the poor."

So intimately is drinking associated with religion that it appears at times as if the right to tipple is divinely sanctioned, upheld if need be by miracles recalling the wedding at Cana. Wulfstan of Winchester, in his *Life of St. Æthelwold*, describes King Eadred's visit to the monastery of Abingdon:

Now it chanced that he had with him not a few of his North-umbrian thegns, and they all accompanied him to the party. The king was delighted, and ordered the guests to be served with lavish draughts of mead. The doors were carefully secured to make sure that no one should get out and be seen to be leaving the royal carousal. Well, the servants drew off drink all day to the hearts' content of the diners, but the level in the container could not be reduced below a palm's measure. The Northumbrians became drunk, as they tend to, and very cheerful they were when they left that evening.

When the lady Æthelflæd finds her supply of mead inadequate for an imminent visit from King Athelstan, she prays to the Virgin, "with the result that the mead never failed, although the butlers served the guests all day with drinking-horns, goblets, and other vessels." When the seventh-century Irish saint Kilian is refused a drink of water by a Frankish noblewoman, he can think of no harsher punishment than to have her beer barrels drained empty by miracle. When she and her husband pursue him with abject apologies and give him land and a new church, the barrels are miraculously refilled. Thirsty Germans throughout western Europe flocked to conversion ceremonies; the real miracle was that, with such a powerful and benevolent new god on tap, it still took Charlemagne thirty years to subdue and Christianize the Old Saxons.

Is it any wonder, then, that the Germans failed to be chastened by their new religion or to respect the sanctity of the holy places? Gregory's own church of St. Martin's was the scene of many a violent encounter. "This Martin of yours, whom you keep quoting in such a fatuous way, means absolutely nothing to us," Frankish soldiers tell a steward seeking to prevent bloodshed in the sanctuary. Eberulf, treasurer to King Chilperic, seeks refuge in St. Martin's from Claudius, his would-be assassin, sent by Chilperic's brother Guntram. Unable to lure Eberulf out into the open, Claudius enters the holy precinct. The two men stab each other before Claudius's servants dash out Eberulf's brains on the paving stones. Eberulf's servants pursue Claudius into the abbot's cell, where they kill him by hurling spears through the window. The abbot himself is dragged from his cell, rioters attack the church, everyone who had sought refuge with Eberulf is killed, the abbot's cell is awash in blood, and the killers loot the church.

The bad example was set from the very height of society and trickled down. It was the royal Frankish custom to divide the realm equally among all male heirs, with the result that brothers and uncles were constantly at each other's throats. King Lothar orders his own son Chramn to be strangled then burnt alive with his entire family in a poor man's hut. King Guntram orders decaying horse dung, wood chips, straw, moldy hay, and stinking mud from the gutters to be flung at his nephew's envoys. King Theuderic sets a trap for his half-brother Lothar, stretching a canvas across the courtyard to conceal the assassins but neglecting to ensure that it reach the floor, with the result that Lothar can see their feet. Overcome with confusion, Theuderic calls off the murder and offers his brother a silver salver, but, regretting his generosity, later sends his son Theudebert to plead for its return. Lothar, magnanimous to a degree that might have surprised the unfortunate Chramn, is happy to comply.

In the midst of such lawlessness and brutality, it is hardly surprising that the ancient practices of hospitality should have been lost and forgotten, especially when recurrent famines often reduced the poor to grinding grape seeds, hazel catkins, or dessicated fern roots for their bread or to selling themselves into slavery in return for food. One story about a civil dispute in Tours, told by Gregory in installments, reads like a particularly nasty soap opera and gives us a fairly good idea of the state of civil society and legal protections among the lower Germanic orders in Gaul in the late sixth century.

It all begins at Christmas time, when a village priest sends his messenger to the home of Austregesil with an invitation to come have a drink. One of Austregesil's men, apparently in his cups already, kills the messenger, provoking the priest's friend Sichar to seek vengeance. Austregesil strikes first, sending a raiding party that kills four of Sichar's servants in his home and makes off with his treasure. Austregesil is found guilty by a tribunal, but Sichar learns that the money is being hidden in the home of the thief's kinsman Auno. With a raiding party of his own, Sichar breaks into Auno's house, kills him, his son, and his brother, and steals his cattle. Bishop Gregory offers Sichar church money to drop the feud, but Auno's son Chramnesind rejects the offer. Sichar heads off to Poitier to seek justice from the king, but en route is wounded by his own slave, whom he had been abusing. Sichar's friends seize the slave, cut off his hands and feet and hang him.

In the meanwhile, Chramnesind, thinking Sichar dead, loots his home, kills his servants, burns down the house, and steals his cattle. For good measure, he also torches the neighbors' homes. He and Sichar are each ordered to pay compensation.

Somehow, Sichar and Chramnesind become great drinking buddies after that, but one sodden night a dispute arises between them and old rancors reemerge. Chramnesind extinguishes the candles, hacks Sichar's skull in half, strips his body, and hangs it naked from a post of the garden fence. Unable to obtain an amnesty from King Childebert because Queen Brunhild had been Sichar's protector, Chramnesind flees briefly to Bourges. But when he makes a second appeal, proving that "he had taken a life in order to avenge an affront" – a perfectly legitimate defense – he is exculpated and all his property is restored.

Ultimately, hard living always takes its toll, and even the restless Germans began to settle down, in a manner of speaking. Not that the ceaseless warfare came to an end; nor that officers of the peace were hired to patrol the streets of Tours; nor even, as far as I know, that the Catholic clergy swore off the bottle and the sword. However, with the exception of the Vikings in the North Sea and the Arabs in Spain, the major national migrations that had precipitated the fall of Rome came to an end. The immediate forebears of the peoples of Western Europe were more or less where they remain to this day. Most of the continent was at least partially evangelized. In Britain, the historian Bede reported in awe that the monasteries were bursting at the seams with retired warriors and that no one stole the brass bowls which King Edwin of Northumbria provided at roadside springs for travelers. And when King Alfred, fleeing the invading Danes, took anonymous shelter in a peasant hut, only to burn the baking loaves that he had been entrusted to watch, the genuine English culinary tradition was born. It can be no coincidence that his countrymen began calling their island Englaland shortly thereafter.

In Gaul, Charlemagne, by all accounts a genuinely devout Christian, set an example of moderation in his habits that was seen and admired by the many foreigners whom he welcomed to his court. Most days he wore the unadorned Frankish national dress of linen shirt, linen breeches, and hose, along with a simple blue cloak in winter. He never drank more than three cups of wine at meals and his suppers consisted of a mere four courses, "not counting the roast." Most important, like Alfred the Great in Wessex a few generations later, he was intellectually voracious and curious, a patron of the arts and letters, importing the finest thinkers from abroad, promoting literacy, and codifying law, although he himself never learned to read. Franks continued to distinguish themselves from Gauls, and Francia itself was long to remain but one of several kingdoms between the Channel and the Mediterranean, but a new era was about to begin. When Charlemagne's grandsons dismantled his empire, Frankish supremacy was irreparably compromised and the erstwhile German overlords began to merge with the far more numerous Gauls to produce the first prototypical Frenchmen, for better or for worse. Western civilization was at last ready for the resumption of traditional hospitality.

Out of the Dark Ages comes the story of one man whose life's arc closely reproduces this maturation process – the emergence of the modern Western European nations from their rough infancy under Germanic tutelage. It is far from certain where, when, or even if this man ever actually lived; even if he did, medieval embellishments of his biography tend to obscure hard facts under layers of romanticizing mythology. The earliest extant accounts of his life date to the early thirteenth century, but tales and legends had been circulating throughout Catholic Europe for centuries prior to that, probably dating back to Frankish Gaul. His story has been told and retold, most recently in Flaubert's *Three Tales*. His legend is depicted in stained glass in the cathedrals of Chartres and Rouen. Chaucer invokes him several times in *The Canterbury Tales*; Gawain prays to him; in England alone, seven ancient churches were dedicated to him. He was Julian, the patron saint of hospitality.

Julian was the beloved only son of a noble couple of the Anjou – in one account, the duke and duchess of Angers themselves. He was a spoiled, callow youth addicted to hunting and given to capricious cruelty to animals. Out hunting one day, and separated from his companions, Julian maliciously wounds a sleeping stag. Before dying, the stag speaks to him, predicting that he will one day kill his own parents. Hoping to avert the prophecy, Julian flees his native country, leaving his grieving parents to believe that he has died.

He eventually makes his way to Jerusalem, where he joins the Knights Hospitallers in valiantly defending the city against the Muslims. On being falsely informed that his father has died, thus freeing him from the prophecy, he heads home but somehow ends up in Galicia, where he defeats a host of Moors besieging a castle. The grateful castellan rewards him with an estate of his own and a beautiful wife, with whom he lives happily for several years.

One day while he is out on the hunt, an old couple arrive at his castle. They are his parents, who have wandered the lands pursuing rumors of his survival. Julian's wife receives them graciously, feeding them and giving them her own bed to rest in. Julian returns from the hunt, sees two figures in the bed and, believing he has caught his wife in adultery, slaughters them as they sleep.

In abject penance, Julian abandons his home and his fortune, followed by his faithful wife. After years of mendicancy, they settle in a hut by a swift stream on the pilgrimage route to Santiago, where they live in exemplary poverty and humility, providing food and shelter to pilgrims and ferrying them across the dangerous current.

One stormy night, a voice calls to them from the far side of the stream. At great peril, Julian crosses the water and greets the traveler, a foul-smelling beggar in filthy rags and such an advanced stage of leprosy that he has lost his nose. Julian grasps him by the thighs and lifts him into the boat, holding him so closely that their lips almost meet and greedily inhaling his pestilent breath in an ecstasy of self-abasement. Back in the hut, Julian and his wife feed their guest and build a roaring fire, but nothing can warm the chill in his bones. Julian tries to revive him with the warmth of his own body, but to no avail. The leper asks Julian's wife to strip and join him in bed, claiming that nothing but the warmth of a woman will do the trick. True to his vow of humility, Julian allows her to fulfill the request, but when she pulls the blanket aside the bed is empty. A voice on the storm announces that their visitor had been none other than Christ in disguise and that Julian is now fully absolved of his sin.

Another seven years they continue to live and toil for the poor, until they are murdered in their beds, like Julian's parents, by a band of passing thieves.

It is not entirely clear why the story of St. Julian the Hospitaller was so immensely popular in the Middle Ages. It certainly incorporates a great many themes of everyday medieval life – religion, the Crusades, pestilence, the dangers of travel, arbitrary violence, the casual cruelty of noblemen, redemption through suffering. I have a suspicion, however, that its popularity lay in the subconscious journey – personal and cultural – that it describes, one that told the people of the Middle Ages both where they had come from and where they saw themselves going.

If we think of Julian as a nation, we can see him starting out on his life's journey as a brutal pagan Frank, Saxon, Visigoth, or Lombard. He is cruel, wantonly destructive, and faithless, but through a series of trials, tests, punishments, and humiliations, he is gradually transformed into the very model of a humble, abject Christian. Certainly, it is hard to picture a hardened Frankish warrior willingly drinking disease from a leper's lips or offering him his naked wife. We tend to imagine the Middle Ages as a place of darkness, fear, ignorance, and superstition, but I doubt that people of those times saw their situation quite so starkly. They had, after all, emerged from an era far darker, more mysterious, and dangerous than theirs, and even among the illiterate there must have been some vague awareness of the deep fog in which their forebears had been enshrouded. Julian was their story, the Frank who became French, the Anglo-Saxon who became English, the Visigoth who became Spanish, the pagan who embraced the true Church.

They could have made him the patron saint of anything: crusaders, ferrymen, lepers, or pimps. Instead, they made him the patron saint of hospitality because his transformation and redemption made possible the reawakening of a forgotten but cherished tradition that had lain dormant for many centuries. Scenes of domesticity, cooking, the life of the peasantry, romance, and the pageantry of noble hospitality had all but disappeared from art and literature under the Germanic hegemony of the Dark Ages. Now, under the divine protection of a new patron, the appurtenances of domestic hospitality were resurgent everywhere, from religious iconography to the emerging vernacular poetry. Hospitality was back in business, just in time for capitalism, colonialism, gunpowder warfare, and the Renaissance.

CHAPTER VII

GAIUS, TITUS, LUCIUS

Must not those who live in kitchens always stink?

Petronius, *Satyricon*

In the history of hospitality, there are those who are invited to the party and those who are not. Those who are not invited participate just as fully in this history as those who are because it is their very absence that defines the opposing camp, since you cannot include someone without excluding someone else. Like ancestral spirits at a shamanistic ritual, those who cannot be seen often make up the majority of those who are present.

You would imagine that those who are invited would be smug, while those who are not would be bitter and insecure. And yet, it is an interesting truth about human nature that this situation tends to arouse bitterness and insecurity on both sides of the fence. Of course, the uninvited may initially experience envy, but pride will usually transmute their bile into jeering contempt and haughtiness, as anyone who has ever watched the Oscars on television will attest. We all know how easy it is to ascribe hubris to others – tragic theater could hardly exist without it.

The bitterness of the invited, however, is a little more complex. You may start out feeling pretty good about yourself, but that won't last unless you're a fool. Instead, you often begin to question the value of inclusion. Am I worthy of being included? Is this company beneath me? Any initial sense of self-satisfaction at being included becomes adulterated with an unstable admixture of guilt, self-doubt, and disdain for one's fellow participants. That, in turn, will probably give rise to self-loathing, resentment of those you rightly suspect of sneering at your participation, and, ultimately, reactionary exclusionism.

I knew these feelings intimately as a child growing up in England. As an American and a Jew, middle-class and intellectual, there was no natural place for me among the confident, athletic, and cosmopolitan children of British, French, Belgian, Persian, and Lebanese aristocrats who peopled my school. I looked down upon their thoughtlessness, their booklessness, their casual obliviousness to self-doubt, while I wanted only to be just like them in every way. Mine was a home of chaos, illness, anxiety, and nonconformity; theirs were places of decorum, serenity, and secure social standing. This made me turn against myself even more scathingly and hate the people I longed for. I was certain that I was smarter than them but that they knew something I could never know. How could they be so calm and sure of themselves otherwise?

I was anything but a misfit. I strove tirelessly, if vainly, to attain a sense of belonging. I cultivated a gift for making friends and never lacked for invitations to country weekends, but I was always lonely in company because I was forever on my guard against being denounced. No one ever outed me, of course, because the harsh searchlight of paranoia makes people (including oneself) appear flatter, more one-dimensional, than they really are. With hindsight, it is clear to me that most of my friends were perfectly decent people who had never scorned me as an insecure wanna-be, but to this very day it is difficult for me to believe that anyone likes me as much as he claims or feigns.

Maybe that's why I keep inviting them over for dinner.

In the year 60, the Roman proconsul to Bithynia was recalled to the capital to serve in the court of the emperor Nero. Not much is known about the life of Titus Petronius Niger – who has also been identified as Gaius Petronius – other than that he was of an extremely wealthy and illustrious family, but what is certain is that he immediately fell into intimate companionship with the emperor, who was in awe of his ability to ally the most refined sophistication to the appearance of unaffected simplicity. Within a year of his arrival, he was distinguished by the extraordinary and unprecedented title of *arbiter elegantiae* – the arbiter of elegance, or master of good taste – giving him the first and final say in all of Nero's aesthetic choices and diversions. "The emperor," says Tacitus, "thought nothing charming or elegant in luxury unless Petronius had expressed to him his approval of it." During his brief ascendancy, Petronius was in full control of coordinating the emperor's banquets, orgies, musical entertainments, games, and guest lists.

But, as men more powerful and ruthless than Petronius were to discover, being close to Nero could be as dangerous as being in his disfavor. The appointment of Ofonius Tigellinus as commander of the Imperial Guard in 62, less than two years after Petronius' return to Rome, marked the beginning of his downfall. Petronius played to Nero's artistic pretensions, Tigellinus to his cruelty; predictably, cruelty won. By 64, Tigellinus was known to be organizing the emperor's banquets and the arbiter's position was becoming increasingly precarious. In 66, Tigellinus implicated Petronius, along with many of Rome's most eminent politicians and intellectuals, including Seneca and Lucan, in the failed plot of Gaius Calpurnius Piso to overthrow Nero. Rather than await the inevitable, Petronius slew himself at Cumae.

Like Seneca and Lucan, Petronius left something for the world to remember him by. Some time between being named Nero's favorite and killing himself, he wrote a masterpiece of prose, a nasty bit of documentary satire that, in its surviving fragments, has come down to us as the ultimate record of decadence at the Roman banquet table. Less obviously, but perhaps more durably as an object lesson, it offers a very revealing insight into the conflicted heart of the real insider, of one who both reviles and is helplessly drawn to the glamor of inclusion, and who suspects that he may have lost himself at the host's elbow. Most critics tend to see Petronius' work as an indictment of Neronian vulgarity and depravity, or at best as an amoral portrait of the nouveau riche. I see it, however, as documenting the efforts of a man to come to terms with his own ambivalence about always being at the top of the A-list. The *Satyricon* is best read not by those who despise the elite and scorn excess, but by those who are secretly attracted to them despite themselves.

Like Americans, Romans of the early empire had a tendency to romanticize their flinty pastoral origins and lost moral rectitude, while viewing their current prosperity as a mixed blessing. Wallowing in ornate decadence, many a Roman poet made an excellent living harking back to the ancestral farmstead with its olive groves, beehives, and virtuous, hardworking, simple-living *Quirites*, who often had to make do with a mere handful of slaves. Almost every patrician had his villa in the Alban hills, Etruria, or Campania where he played the humble homesteader, raising his own vintages, eating homegrown bread and cheese. Every soldier recalled the glorious triumphs of bygone days, when *real* Romans were the army's backbone and you came home after a hard-fought campaign to hear Latin being spoken on the streets of the capital, instead of this bastardized babble of Greek, Gaulish, Syrian, German, and Hebrew. Like Americans, Roman orators at the pinnacle of Rome's power enjoyed nothing quite so much as to lean on the crutch of patriotism while predicting the imminent swamping of the *patria* in debauchery, corruption, sloth, and indulgence. When the poet Horace, in the very opening years of the empire, bemoaned the glory days when "private estates were small, and great was the common weal," he was only reiterating in sublime Latin what was being said in coarse vernacular on every street corner and from the speakers' stump in every forum.

Nero's villa, the *Domus Aurea*, or Golden House, was the epitome of all that ordinary Romans had come to despise in their degenerate rulers. It replaced the *Domus Transitoria*, partially destroyed in the great fire of 64, which was said to have been started and fanned by the henchmen of Tigellinus in order to clear the central city for Nero's monumental dream house. Whether or not the fire was set intentionally, the Golden House and its grounds were built precisely atop the three neighborhoods that had been entirely leveled. The estate covered some two hundred acres on the Palatine and Oppian hills and spanned the entire valley to the Esquiline. The grounds centered on a vast artificial lake and boasted temples, vineyards, pastures, orchards, and herds of wild beasts – a veritable *rus in urbe*. The estate kept growing, eating away at the city; a popular song, claiming that "Rome is becoming one house," advised Romans to flee to Veii, "if that house does not soon seize upon Veii as well." The palace itself, an oversized Mediterranean peristyle villa, had a triple colonnade running along its entire length (which Suetonius asserts to have spanned a mile) and in the vestibule a statue of Nero more than one hundred feet tall (the *colossus* after which the Colosseum was named). Pliny claims that the entire façade was gilded. The house had two bathing pools, one of salt water, the other of sulfur, and an enormous ramp of running water to cool the air in the dining room. Nero plundered all of Greece to furnish its 150 rooms. The walls were encrusted with marble, gold, gems, mother-of-pearl; the mosaics on the vaulted ceilings played out epic scenes from Greek mythology. "There were dining-rooms with fretted ceilings of ivory, whose panels could turn and shower down flowers and were fitted with pipes for sprinkling the guests with perfumes. The main banquet hall was circular and constantly revolved day and night, like the heavens." The *Domus Aurea* was not quite complete at Nero's death in 68, but he was able to live and entertain there for several years, at its dedication saying merely that "he was at last beginning to be housed like a human being."

No one was quite able to pinpoint the moment at which old-fashioned Roman virtue had succumbed, but historians, moralists, and poets spoke with one voice in naming the perfidious Orient as its killer. The Greeks had been infected by the arts of luxury from conquered Persia and had passed on the disease to Rome, where it incubated and spread throughout the second and first centuries B.C. Pliny could not say it plainly enough: "The conquest of Asia . . . introduced luxury here." He despised such Asiatic luxury, as did Horace, Martial, Strabo, Livy, and anyone else who sought to score an easy hit with the disaffected. Crankiness aside, they weren't entirely wrong. The Romans were indeed irrepressible assimilators; they copied or adapted Hellenic styles of poetry, history, writing, architecture, worship, and mythology. One did not necessarily have to be a reactionary to consider the secondary consequences of colonialism upon Roman society and morals to be less than salutary. No sooner had they conquered the Greek colonies in southern Italy and Sicily than *liquamen* – the Roman version of the salty fish condiment *garos* – became ubiquitous in their cooking. The modern addiction to expensive wine, Phrygian marble, Persian nard, Indian mushrooms, Cyrenaican silphium, Egyptian cotton, slave labor, sodomy, gold, and, ultimately, autocrats was simply a nasty virus the Romans had contracted in their travels. Seneca tells with puritan dismay of how Apicius (one of several Apicii to whom the famous cookbook is ascribed), having squandered one hundred million sesterces on banquets, and with only ten million left, killed himself rather than risk starving to death. Real Romans killed themselves for honor, not dinner.

When it came to setting precedents for depravity, the Romans were awfully diligent and inventive, but too much has been written about Roman excess – especially in food and sex – to make it worth retelling here at any great length. Still, it's hard to resist, especially when writing about hospitality, and even more especially when the excesses of the early emperors make today's ill-omened headlines read like excerpts from a provincial crime blotter.

The Romans' appetite for self-indulgence was whetted under the empire, and grew progressively sharper under the first five emperors, the so-called Julio-Claudian dynasty. Rome had had dictators before, under the republic, but these were appointed by the Senate during military emergencies for fixed terms of six months (the fighting season) and were generally, with a few notable exceptions, in no position to abuse their limited power. In principle, even the imperator was nothing more than a high-ranking magistrate subordinate to the Senate, but that was a mere technicality. No senator was going to keep Augustus, Tiberius,

Caligula, Claudius, or Nero from his Asiatic luxuries.

Julius Caesar was the founder of the line but is not included because he never assumed the title imperator. This is just as well for any study of imperial depravity, for his worst crime against hospitality seems to have been to have put his baker in irons for serving one kind of bread to Caesar and another kind to Caesar's guests. Marcus Cato summed it up well when he called Caesar "the only man who undertook to overthrow the state when sober."

His adopted son Octavian, later Augustus, the first Roman emperor, was almost as restrained. Although he loved to gamble and enjoyed hosting banquets, he could be very choosy about his guests and was known to be a frugal eater and drinker. Indeed, he often ate before his guests arrived, showed up late at table, and then withdrew early – tendencies that, while not criminal, were not necessarily those of an attentive host. Later in life, however, he began to exhibit tentative signs of the behavorial patterns that would be so successfully developed and refined by his successors. Scandalously effeminate in his youth, he became a notorious adulterer in maturity, going so far, while dining at the home of one senator, to seduce the man's wife in his presence, "bringing her back to the table with her hair in disorder and her ears glowing." In the midst of a dire famine, he once held the notorious "supper of the twelve Gods" at which he blasphemously assumed the role of Apollo. These incidents, while only modestly reprehensible by the standards soon to be set, were specifically cited as precedents for much worse in the years to come. He was the only Julio-Claudian emperor whose death was not openly celebrated by the people of Rome.

His stepson and successor, Tiberius, continued the gradual downward trend. Early in his career, for reasons that are not entirely clear, he undertook a voluntary eight-year exile in Rhodes, where he lived a life of extraordinary privacy and where, perhaps, he picked up many of the habits that he took with him when he later retired from active statecraft. He was a humble, if laconic, ruler, prone to depression, more austere than author-itative – "mud kneaded with blood," his own tutor called him. He built no public monuments and held few games. Despite having exerted every effort (including murder) to secure the title, he was always more comfortable in a private setting than in a public one. In the spirit of his dynasty, he despised and tormented the members of his immediate family, driving his own daughter-in-law Agrippina to starve herself to death.

In the year 26, about halfway through his reign, he left Rome, never to return, and fell back on Capri, where one Titus Caeso-nius Priscus reigned as Master of the Imperial Pleasures – a sort of beta version of *Arbiter Elegantiae*. On Capri, Tiberius was able to give free rein to his vices, the least of which was an inordinate thirst. His villa was a veritable museum of pornography, while teams of male and female prostitutes roamed the woods and groves of his estate, ready to solicit or perform with each other at his pleasure. He trained young boys, his "little fishes," to dart around him as he swam, nibbling and licking his imperial parts. He was particularly fond of fellatio, not only demanding it of high-born female guests but also coaxing it out of unweaned babies.

His cruelty and cold-bloodedness thrived and blossomed in the balmy island climate. He found the very loveliest spot on the island, commanding spectacular views of the exquisite Bay of Naples, from which he delighted in watching his torture victims flung to their death. One of his favorite pranks was to ply his male guests with copious draughts of wine, then have them seized and their penises tightly bound with cord.

He was succeeded by his great-nephew Gaius, more commonly known as Caligula. Caligula reigned for a mere four years, but in that time did much to advance the Julio-Claudian marriage of hospitality and cruelty. It was under Caligula that accepting the emperor's hospitality became a game of Russian roulette in earnest. Forcing senators to wait on him, "napkin in hand at either end of his couch," he would laugh loudly at the thought that he could have their throats cut at any moment. He was an eager poisoner and, like Tiberius, enjoyed watching torture, most especially at mealtime. He perpetuated the Augustan tradition of seducing his senators' wives and enjoyed incestuous relations with all his sisters, whom he elevated above his own wife at the banquet table. He once forced a man to attend his own son's execution, then threw him a banquet to cheer him up. He sincerely believed in his own divinity, was an occasional cross-dresser, and liked to walk barefoot on carpets of gold coins. He was finally struck down by members of his own bodyguard and succeeded by his uncle Claudius.

By the time of Claudius' accession in 41, most of the family traits were firmly entrenched. Although an accomplished scholar, Claudius was every bit the profligate host, gambler, drunk, glutton, lecher, and audience for torture as his forebears. He was an inveterate vomiter and issued an edict encouraging flatulence at table, "quietly or noisily." His charms were complemented by a tendency to foam at the mouth and trickle at the nose when upset. He is largely held to have been poisoned with tainted mushrooms at a family meal, allegedly by his wife, Agrippina, on behalf of her son by a previous marriage, sixteen-year-old Lucius Domitius Ahenobarbus. Whatever the circumstances of Claudius' death, young Lucius, under his adoptive name Nero, was acclaimed emperor in 54.

It will be fairly clear by now that Nero descended from a

champion line and was destined to fulfill the promise of his ancestors. His natural father, Domitius, who killed one of his own freedmen "for refusing to drink as much as he was ordered," accurately predicted that nothing good could be hoped of the offspring of such parents. His mother had the foresight to prevent him from studying philosophy, which she considered a burden to any future ruler. Just to make certain, she entrusted his early education to a dancer and a barber – and sure enough, Lucius was equal parts artist and cutthroat. His later tutor, Seneca, for all his moral stature and carefully crafted Epicurean brand of stoicism, could do nothing with him and let him run wild in the deluded hope that the boy would burn himself out. Again, too much has already been said of Nero's crimes. What else, after all, could be expected from a self-anointed musical genius whose three favorite songs were "Orestes the Matricide," "The Blinding of Oedipus," and "The Frenzy of Hercules"?

It might be useful even so to look into the annals of Nero's home life and hospitality, in which he perfected and surpassed the clumsy beginnings of his predecessors. Like them, he reveled in a good poisoning, which, like them, he preferred to witness firsthand at the dining table. Thus, he watched impassively as his brother Britannicus died horribly at a family luncheon. The good prefect Burrus, who had been highly instrumental in his accession to empire, he dispatched with a toxic throat medicine, replacing him with the venomous Tigellinus. At the dining table he murdered friend and foe alike – "a number are known to have been slain all together at a single meal along with their preceptors and attendants." Three attempts were made to poison his mother, with whom he was rumored to be incestuously involved; when these failed, he sought to drown her in an elaborately booby-trapped ship, and when she managed against all odds to swim safely to shore, he lost all patience with her and had her run through with swords. When the opened veins of his first wife, Octavia, failed to kill her fast enough, she was suffocated in a hot vapor bath. In a fit of pique, he kicked his pregnant second wife, Poppaea Sabina, to death, then regretfully honored her memory by castrating the slave boy Sporus (who bore an unfortunate resemblance to the martyred woman) and marrying him ceremoniously. Thus, Nero could proudly claim the fourfold portfolio of parricide, fratricide, matricide, and regicide. It is hardly any wonder that, like Augustus, he considered himself the living incarnation of Apollo.

Almost as atrocious as his crimes against family and hospitality were those he committed against music. He scandalized all of Rome not only by his appearances on the professional stage but also by his dreadful voice and mediocre lyre playing, which he inflicted on all and sundry, proudly and indiscriminately, in public and private settings alike. Tacitus says in wry understatement that his poems "lack vigour, inspiration, and homogeneity." He competed in musical competitions with apparently sincere trepidation, although no one was permitted to win but him and the statues of previous victors were torn down and dragged away. As it was forbidden to leave any theater while Nero played, women were known to give birth during his performances, while others risked life and limb by leaping from the closed gates or feigned death in order to escape. It was probably not hyperbolic for Cassius Dio to claim that everyone "regarded the dead as fortunate."

This, then, was the history and reality of the imperial household to which Petronius found himself summoned from the depths of Asia Minor in the year 60. As an educated and erudite man, he was certainly intimately familiar with that history. As an aristocrat with impeccable social connections, he must have been well informed of all of the gossip and known most of its subjects personally, including the emperor. As a worldly slave-owner, he had had ample opportunity to indulge in many of the same luxuries and vices. As a former soldier, he was no stranger to bloodshed, betrayal, and intrigue. On all these counts, it is impossible not to believe that he knew just what he was getting into and the kind of people he would have to deal with when he set out to make himself indispensable to Nero. In fact, it may even be fair to say that he should have been able to foresee the fate that awaited him. He could undoubtedly have avoided it by maintaining a low profile and safe distance from the court; he was wealthy and accomplished enough not to need to put himself in the way of such dangerous patronage. And yet, by all evidence, he plunged headlong into the lion's den and eagerly sought out its darkest recesses. Why did he do it? What could he possibly have had to gain when he had so much to lose?

The brief but incisive portrait of Petronius by Tacitus is full of telling contradictions. On the one hand, he was said to be a man who spent his days in sleep and his nights in self-indulgence; on the other, he is reported to have been an energetic and canny administrator in Bithynia. "Indolence had raised him to fame, as energy raises others," but he cannot possibly have achieved his meteoric rise as Nero's confidante and guide merely by the example of his indolence – he must have worked hard and cunningly to do it. He was *"erudito luxu"* – learned in luxury, a delicious oxymoron – but was never ranked among the herd of debauchees and spendthrifts, "like most of those who squander their substance." He somehow managed to set himself apart from and above the common sycophants and self-seekers – most pointedly and at manifest risk from the thuggish Tigellinus – and still cultivate a reputation for casual and catholic charm. "His talk and his doings, the freer they were and the more show of carelessness they exhibited, were the better liked, for their look of natural simplicity." From Tacitus emerges the picture of a complicated and clever man who succeeded in placing self-gratification and aesthetic principles at the service of his political ambitions. Unlike Tigellinus and other political operatives of Nero's household, whose lusts and ruthlessness are nakedly exposed for all eternity, Petronius remains opaque in his motives and ultimate beliefs and convictions. The otherwise gimlet-eyed Plutarch could not see beyond his superficial charge against Petronius as a mere flatterer, while, for all his insight, Tacitus is completely stumped as to whether the arbiter was indulging a true taste for vice or merely affecting it. Petronius may have imagined that such opacity guaranteed his safety as one of Nero's favored guests and companions.

In *Quo Vadis*, Henryk Sienkiewicz portrays Petronius – whom he calls Gaius – as a self-serving, world-weary cynic without morals or conviction. Unfortunately, Petronius' principal function in the story is to serve as a foil to his nephew Vinicius as he undergoes a soul-shattering conversion to Christianity. The last thing I would want to do is to impugn the early Christian martyrs, but in his zeal to contrast them to the unredeemed pagans, Sienkiewicz got Petronius all wrong, including his given name.

The entire subject of Petronius' inner soul would be sterile had he not left a testament to himself. Some historians believe that the *Satyricon* was written at the height of his influence as a kind of unpublished amusement for the members of the court. This is unlikely for a number of reasons, the most obvious being that it could not have failed to incur the imperial wrath had it come to Nero's attention. In the year 62, Aulus Didius Gallus Fabricius Veiento was found guilty of insulting senators and priests and all his books were burned; we can only imagine what Nero would have done to a lampooner of his divine self and company.

Another reason to believe that Petronius kept the *Satyricon* more or less to himself during his lifetime is that by far the most scathing and damning episode, Trimalchio's banquet, was not discovered until the mid-seventeenth century, when a later transcription was found in a small village on the coast of Dalmatia. How was this section of the book preserved intact when so much of the manuscript is almost certainly lost forever? It is not implausible that, for reasons of self-preservation, Petronius kept the Trimalchio chapter sequestered, separate from the rest of the novel and safely hidden from the gossips and professional informers who infested the imperial court.

Because of the fragmentary nature of its surviving portions, there is not much of a discernible plot to the *Satyricon*. In the convention of Menippean satire, it parodies contemporary philosophical thought, partly in verse, partly in prose. It is especially harsh on rhetoricians. The story follows the adventures and misadventures of the student Encolpius; Giton, his beautiful slave boy and lover; and Ascyltos, his friend and sometimes bitter rival for Giton's affections. They argue and part; they meet up again and reconcile; Giton abandons Encolpius for Ascyltos, then returns; they encounter the poet Eumolpus, who is viciously assailed for the mediocrity of his verse; they are attacked, seduced, enslaved, and freed; Encolpius suffers a debilitating and humiliating bout of impotence that is ultimately cured by a sorceress. The book begins in midsentence and ends in midsentence. The longest continuous episode of the book is that in which Encolpius and Ascyltos, through their teacher Agamemnon, are invited to supper at the home of the enormously wealthy freedman Trimalchio. The meal is attended mostly by the host's aging cronies, who, like him, are poorly educated former slaves who have made good. Trimalchio is tirelessly, epically vulgar. Throughout the night, he and his guests talk about little but money, how to get it and how to spend it. His household gods are Gain, Luck, and Profit. At one point, he has his bookkeeper read out the daily profit sheet from his estates, including the birth of seventy slaves, five hundred thousand pecks of wheat put up in the barn, five hundred oxen broken in, and ten million sesterces locked up in the strongbox. Trimalchio boasts loudly of his constipation, cured by "suppository of pomegranate-rind and pine sap boiled in vinegar." He discusses in great detail the design of his future tomb, to be engraved with scenes of the entire town carousing at his table and to be inscribed prominently with the epitaph "HE NEVER ONCE LISTENED TO A PHILOSOPHER!" He thinks it the very height of sophistication to have his slaves sing as they serve, but, for all his efforts, the entertainment is dismissed as "low cabaret." Like prompters at a sitcom, the servants must lead the audience in clapping.

The fare served up is as excessive as the host. A partial list of appetizers includes roast dormice sprinkled with honey and poppyseeds; Syrian plums and pomegranate seeds; fig-peckers marinated in peppered egg yolk and stuffed into peahen eggs; testicles and kidneys; cheese tarts; lobster; sow's udder; and snapper in pepper sauce. A wild boar is roast, stuffed with live quail, and garnished with cake piglets. A roast pig is brought in and the cook threatened with a beating for having forgotten to gut it; but when he proceeds to slit it open before the horrified company, it disgorges a cascade of cooked sausages and giblets. For dessert, cakes and fruits are served suffused with saffron; pastry thrushes are stuffed with nuts and raisins; quinces are adorned with thorns to look like sea urchins.

No reader, ancient or modern, can fail to recognize in Trimalchio the eternal nouveau riche, who has the means to inspire envy but inspires equal contempt for his lack of subtlety and the low-bred company he keeps. Nothing has changed in two thousand years to soften or mitigate that portrait – only recently the *Times* carried the story of six bankers who treated themselves to sixty-two thousand dollars' worth of vintage Pétrus at one meal. Each one of us probably carries with him the image of some news-making plutocrat whose money and gorgeous arm-candy he delights in despising. We sneer at his greed but cannot help imagining ourselves in his place, consoling ourselves that we would know the best and most tasteful ways of spending his riches if we had them. We might even imagine that we deserve them more than one who puts them to such vulgar use. We flatter ourselves with the understated simplicity of our own tastes and picture ourselves, invited to the ball, rejecting the garish display and all it represents.

Few critics doubt that, in the words of one, "the prototypes of the guests at Trimalchio's table were almost certainly actual people known to Nero no less than to Petronius." We will never know, of course, whether certain characters correspond specifically to courtiers of the author's acquaintance, but that is irrelevant. No one would suggest, either, that Trimalchio is an explicit portrait of Nero, but the similarities between them would have been more than enough to cost Petronius his life if the emperor had chanced to read the manuscript. There is, of course, their shared aversion to philosophers. Both are wildly profligate and believe that a man is at least partly defined and ennobled by his willingness to spend recklessly. Suetonius' description of Nero – "He thought that there was no other way of enjoying riches and money than by riotous extravagance, declaring that only stingy and niggardly fellows kept a correct account of what they spent, while fine and genuinely magnificent gentlemen wasted and squandered" – readily applies to Trimalchio. Both were shameless exhibitionists with terrible voices; both shared a keen and well-informed interest in architecture. Both preserved their first beards in golden caskets. Both had dining rooms with mechanical ceilings that opened to shower gifts and perfume on their guests. Both had a decided penchant for scenting the soles of their feet. I think it's fair to assume that no one in Nero's court was ever offered the opportunity to read the *Satyricon*.

The thing about Trimalchio is that, for all his trumpishness, we cannot help but like him, as Petronius clearly intended us to. He is brash, coarse, and temperamental, but he is also unapologetically himself, larger than life, a carousing Bacchus, a hungry maw, still greedy at an advanced age for everything life has to offer. He is unstintingly generous to friends and strangers alike and enjoys a surprisingly casual and empathetic give-and-take relationship with his slaves. He has triumphed over terrible odds and come away with an unsentimental but not at all bitter assessment of the rules of the game: "Take my word for it, if you have a penny you're worth a penny, you are valued for just what you have." Contrast this philosophy with Nero's darker conviction that "no man was chaste or pure in any part of his body, but that most of them concealed their vices and cleverly drew a veil over them; and that therefore he pardoned all other faults in those who confessed to him their lewdness" and it becomes obvious that if Trimalchio is a stand-in for the emperor, he is one with all the mercurial cruelty, madness, and blood-lust bleached out of him.

Every paradox of Petronius' personality and the dangerous choices he knowingly made come together and are illuminated by Trimalchio. It seems obvious that, since the book cannot have been read by many, if any, of its contemporaries, it was written as a kind of self-exorcism – part expiation, part wishful thinking – a drawn-out analytical exercise in which the author is attempting to understand and justify his own impulses and conflicting desires. Petronius does not need Nero, his money, his influence, or his protection; he sneers at the emperor's crude depravity, artistic mediocrity, and lack of aesthetic refinement; he finds no intellectual peers at court. And yet he is not only attracted by the emperor's hospitality and intimacy, but also actually co-opts them to his own mortal peril. Is it a fatal addiction to debauchery that killed him or a fatal addiction to observing debauchees? Excess or introspection? Gaius or Titus? Either way, he can't help himself, but he can feel terribly confused by his own conflicting desires. They inspire shame, self-reproach, anger. Which is better: intellectual sophistication or naked power and the freedom to wield it? He can't compare himself to Nero, who is a fiend and does not offer a useful foil, but he can contrast himself without guilt to Trimalchio, who represents all the forbidden attractions without the atrocity. Trimalchio is the Frankenstein monster, created from Nero's body parts once the vicious heart, diseased mind, and incestuous loins have been discarded. Because he is likable and his vices are generous, Trimalchio makes it ethically permissible for Petronius to be perverse. Unlike Nero, he is the moralist's vulgarian. If Petronius can look at the emperor, his host and boss, and see Trimalchio, he can remain at court, indulge his pleasures, and still distance himself morally from the orgy of blood.

On the very first page of the *Satyricon*, Agamemnon poses a rhetorical question: "Must not those who live in kitchens always stink?" I imagine that this was the question that haunted Petronius throughout his years – the good along with the bad – as guest and dean of the *Domus Aurea*. It is easy to see him harassed by it, waking up in a cold sweat in the middle of the afternoon; pondering it solemnly in his bath as the fading light and muffled din of the Roman evening wafted in on a dusty breeze; shaking it off as he set out in his chair for yet another long night of pleasure (or feigned pleasure) at the palace. Maybe it came back to him as his retinue glided through the palace gates while the guards held back the throngs of beggars, petitioners, and onlookers at spear-point. Maybe he heard it again later as he reclined on his dining couch in Nero's banquet hall, deep in his cups in the dark hours, as a slave girl anointed the soles of his feet with scented oil and the ceiling disgorged flower petals and perfume and the artificial stars revolved through the artificial sky overhead. "Must not those who live in kitchens always stink?" It must have been exhilarating and terrifying for him to see those words written down for the first time, a rebuke that had taken almost a lifetime in the formulating. Finding the answer to the charge was the challenge he set for himself in the final years of his life, in his work and in his death. *Is* there any way at all to live in the kitchen and not be a stinker? One way or another, it's a question we might all stand to ask ourselves a little more often.

The life of a Roman aristocrat was largely a preparation for his death. A good death was the crowning glory of a life well led and the sole necessary act of redemption for a flawed one. All contemporary philosophy and education, as epitomized in Senecan stoicism, was geared toward instilling a fearlessness of death, an assiduous cultivation of personal dignity, and a contempt for superstition that, if often set aside in the frenzy of debauch and intrigue, were readily available, more often than not, at the moment of truth. This was especially true of patricians, for whom the option of suicide was an envied privilege in the execution of a death sentence. The death of Socrates, of course, was the standard by which all suicides were judged. If you ranked a mention in the histories or annals, or merely a fleeting hiccup in the marketplace of gossip, you could be certain that your suicide would eventually be set up and assessed – occasionally favorably, but usually not – against that of Socrates. It happened to every principal actor in this chapter, each one a suicide.

First to go was Seneca in 65, a conspirator in the plot to assassinate his former student (which failed, incidentally, only because Piso refused to kill Nero in his own villa, since "to stain the sanctity of hospitality with the blood of an emperor, however evil, would cause a bad impression"). Having waffled egregiously and somewhat hypocritically on his moral duty throughout his life, Seneca proceeded to death in much the same manner. After delivering his final orations and dictating his final musings, he hesitates several times (ostensibly out of sensitivity to his wife, who has begged to be allowed to join him in death) before he opens the arteries at his wrists. The blood spills too slowly, so he slices at the veins in his legs and knees. Even so, the process is "tedious" and he drinks poison – the same drug, his chronicler insists on pointing out, used by the condemned in Athens. When that fails, too, he has himself carried into a bath and suffocates in the steam. An alternate account has him surviving this, too, and having to be finished off by soldiers. It is an honorable end, aspiring to but falling well short of the benchmark, lacking in resolve, dignity, and pacing, much like his life.

Nero died by his own hand in 68 as the troops of the rebel general Galba entered the city. One need hardly read Suetonius' account to imagine its substance. In the middle of the night, barefoot in a tunic, Nero throws on an old cloak, covers his face, and flees for the suburbs. He scrambles on all fours through the undergrowth, tearing his clothes and skin, before reaching the humble refuge of a freedman's villa. Touchingly, among the very few who remain with him is his "wife" Sabina, the renamed slave boy Sporus whom he had had castrated to replace Poppaea. He rests on a filthy straw mattress in a slave's room before summoning up the nerve to stab himself in the throat, uttering an autoeulogy that will echo down the ages: "What an artist the world is losing!" Until the very end, Nero entertained hopes of being spared to make his way out into the world as an itinerant professional musician.

Tigellinus, predictably, sought to betray Nero the moment Galba entered Rome, placing his Praetorian Guards at the new emperor's service. But he botched the surrender, resulting in his own arrest and the slaughter of some seven thousand guards. Family connections saved him for the moment, but when Galba fell to his rival Otho barely seven months later, Tigellinus' time was up. Surrounded by his mistresses in the public baths of Sinuessa, he shamefully prevaricated until finally slashing his throat with a razor – an unseemly blade no patrician would ever have chosen – "still further defiling a notorious life by a tardy and ignominious death."

For Petronius, no less than for the others, the death is a commentary on the life. But because very nearly the sum total of our knowledge of the historical Petronius is confined to two paragraphs in Book XVI of Tacitus' *Annals*, it is much more than that. Besides the *Satyricon*, these five hundred words are our only window into his mind and heart. The death must do more than cap the life; it must represent the life metonymically. And what a death it is.

Petronius is following the emperor to Campania but is detained at his villa in Cumae. He does not need to be told what his house arrest portends and decides that it is time to abandon fear and hope alike. He declines to be hurried, however. His death, like his life, is to be an orchestrated and choreographed entertainment for his friends, who are all present. He opens his wrists then binds them up again, so that he might regulate the bloodletting and enjoy the full measure of his ebbing hours. He engages his guests in casual conversation, steering it ever away from serious thoughts and from the temptation to wax heroic to which Seneca had succumbed. Everything is to be light and pleasant. His guests, in turn, recite for him, "not thoughts on the immortality of the soul or on the theories of philosophers, but light poetry and playful verses." It is presumably during these moments that he allows the blood to flow, perhaps in a side room or bath so as not to upset his guests. He returns to lavish gifts upon his slaves, freeing many. Because he leaves behind no wife or child who will need protection, he dictates a detailed account of every secret of Nero's depravity to which he has been privy and sends it under seal to the emperor. He then breaks his signet ring so that it cannot be misused after he is gone. He binds up his wounds yet again as they sit down to dinner, as it would not become a conscientious host to spill blood on the dining table. The fare is modest but sublime, all the best that the waters of Cumae have to offer: oysters, mussels, black and white sea acorns, raw spondyli in vinegar; maybe Petronius indulges his weakness for sow's udder and aged Falernian. As the dessert dishes are being cleared away, he reaches for one of his favorite objects, a beautiful myrrhine ladle worth more than three hundred thousand sesterces, and smashes it to the ground, unable to bear the thought that it might find its way into the emperor's possession. It is his only moment of melodrama and he smiles sheepishly, sorry not for himself but for the ruined ladle. Then, having eaten and drunk his fill, heard a last song or two, Petronius kisses his friends good night and takes himself off to bed, just as he might on any night, so that "death, though forced on him, might have a natural appearance."

The death of Petronius Arbiter is a fairly seminal text for classical historians, but I have never understood why it is not more commonly known and retold. There are few deaths in all of literature, let alone history, to rival it for elegance, dignity,

thoughtful humor, courage, generosity, tact, worldly sophistication, and philosophical consistency. It's hard enough to pull off
the kind of beautiful death that all men must admire, envy, and
strive to emulate; to do so while graciously hosting an evening of
delicious food, delightful conversation, and pleasant entertainment may be an achievement unique in the annals of human
civilization.

It should also be pointed out, in case it is not perfectly obvious,
that Petronius' death was every bit a martyrdom. He died because
he had dedicated his life to the pursuit of truth and the truth
ended up pursuing him. He wanted to know, needed to know,
had to understand, at peril to his own life and soul, what happens
to a person when all his fantasies of inclusion are fulfilled. Most
of us are privileged to participate in only a fraction of the
entertainments to which we imagine we might like to be invited;
in turn, we have no access to many people we imagine we might
care to invite to our own. We are saved by this exclusion; it makes
us humble, judicious, optimistic, inventive. Imagine if you were
suddenly invited to all the most glorious parties and glamorous
homes in the world. It doesn't have to be vulgar – no swimming
pools or movie stars – it just has to be your fantasy: the intimate
dinners of a revered biochemist; a private recital by your favorite
soprano; after-hours drinks in the Oval Office; the pope's birth-
day party. You are welcome everywhere, anytime. Everybody
wants to be your friend, to be you; everybody envies, hates
you. How much of you survives? Do you really believe you
are strong enough to resist the gravitational force of temptation?
Are you really stronger, smarter, humbler, more detached, more
self-aware, more cynical, more intellectual than all those idiots in
the gossip columns, in *Dan's Papers*, on *Entertainment Tonight*, in
black tie at the Stockholms Stadshus for the Nobel banquet? The
only way you will ever know if you are better than the people you

envy is to put yourself in harm's way and take your chances. The stakes are high: if you are no better, you lose your soul; if you are better, you lose your life.

Fortunately, there is no need to put yourself to the test. Petronius sacrificed himself to save you. He assumed all the world's burdens of celebrity, vanity, unlimited self-indulgence, and depravity, and embraced his martyrdom so you would not have to. Today, when we are tempted by or envious of some thing or event from which we have been excluded, solace is available in the form of a simple formula: What Would Petronius Do?

CHAPTER VIII

FRIENDLY TO STRANGERS

*For what other reason would a man pray to the gods to give him wealth
and abundance of means, than that he may help his friends and sow the
harvest of gratitude, that sweet goddess? For in drinking and eating we
all take the same pleasure; but it needs not rich feasts to quell hunger.*
Athenaeus of Naucratis, *Deipnosophistae*

Sometimes, in the quiet moments just before the first guest
arrives, I find myself suddenly paralyzed by fear. I stop what I
am doing and look about the room. Is there something I have
forgotten to do? I run through a mental checklist of the menu.
No, every course is fully prepared and accounted for. The table is
set, silver polished, linens folded and in place. Wine is chilling in
the refrigerator, vodka in the freezer. The CD changer is filled. All
the lightbulbs are working, all the invitations accepted. The TV is
off and the girls are in the bath. Nothing is out of order, yet
something feels terribly wrong. What am I missing?

A lot of people I know are afraid all the time. We all share many
of the same worries over our jobs, our own or our children's
health, our savings, our success, our own worth, our sex lives,
our spouse's ongoing interest, or our lack of a partner. But there
is also an underlying, less specific fear – what some might call an
ontological or existential anxiety – that shrouds our days and
seeps into our dreams. We feel empty and seek meaning. We

yearn, and know not what we yearn for. There is a black hole at the center of our understanding that engulfs and crushes our every attempt to explore it. Something is missing.

You are a footsoldier in Agamemnon's army camped before the walls of Troy. You live in an almost constant state of hunger, filth, exhaustion, and irritability. You have been fighting for almost ten years now, laying waste the once green plain, engaging in skirmishes and the occasional pitched battle with the Asiatics, who show no sign of weakening. For almost ten years, you have slept on the hard shingle or in the beached ships, enduring untold hardships and privation. Not a day goes by that you do not cast a longing gaze across the sea toward your home, your little farm on the gentle slopes of Boeotia.

How you miss all the food you once took so for granted, available in such abundance in your orchards and fields and the surrounding lands! The cherries, persimmons, grapes, damsons, figs, melons, almonds, quinces, and myrtle berries; the asparagus, artichokes, radishes, chickpeas, cucumbers, mallow, and truffles; the barley cakes, honey cakes, cheesecakes, and sesame cakes; the snails and eggs and milk; the thrushes, finches, titmice, ringdoves, quail, finches, and blackbirds. When was the last time you had an olive – a simple, humble olive?

More than anything, you miss the fish and mollusks drawn in such delightful profusion at all times of the year from local waters, eaten with such relish at every meal. It has been so long you can barely remember what they taste like, the mussels, oysters, bear crabs, scallops, clams, sea squirts; moray, conger, and electric eels ("the king of everything associated with a feast," goes the well-known saying); small fry, anemones, gilthead, and sea bream, parrot wrasse, hake, boar fish, thresher, and sawtoothed sharks, pig fish, lobster, shrimp, bullhead, lyre fish, turbot, tuna, bonito, mackerel, swordfish, parrot fish, red and gray mullet, monkfish, ray, angler, and octopus. All for the asking! They practically jumped into the nets!

How ironic, that you should be camped out for ten years on the beach and never taste a fish. How ironic and cruel. The plain above the beach has been reduced to dust by the marauding armies and the livestock must be raised or rustled miles away then shipped or herded back to the Greek camps through hostile territory, yet all you and your fellows ever get to eat is lamb and goat, goat and lamb, roasted unseasoned on spits, a little wild boar when it is available, and the occasional beef on holy days. And why? It's all because of the fickle gods! You are careful not to complain out loud, and you try not to even think such blasphemous thoughts, but everybody on that godforsaken beach – with the possible exception of Menelaus, who is determined to get his wife back and is fully convinced that his quest is divinely ordained – feels exactly the way you do. You are all heartily sick and tired of having to cater to the gods' every whim.

The gods are everywhere, walking among you, watching your every move, meddling in your most trivial affairs for their own amusement, sniffing out the least impiety and punishing it. You can be sure that every time there is a violent downpour, or a setback on the battlefield, or a shipwreck, or a drought, or a thunderstorm, or a death by illness, or a spring tide forcing the boats to be hauled up in the middle of the night, someone somewhere did something to displease some god. You can take nothing for granted when it comes to the gods because they are so moody and changeable and childish, and there are so many of them and so few with firm allegiances. You can do nothing, nothing at all, without first ascertaining that some god won't be offended.

Most exasperating of all, you can put nothing in your mouth

without first dedicating a portion of it to the gods. And it so happens that the gods don't care for fish. All they want from humans is wine and the greasy smoke from burning animal fat, which rises to Olympus and pleases their nostrils. No other sacrifice will satisfy them. And so, in order to leave nothing to chance on the battlefield, the armies of the Greeks and of the Trojans have eaten nothing but red meat for the past ten years. And you are still no closer to getting inside the Trojan walls than you were when you first arrived.

You have no way of knowing this, but hundreds of years from now – long after Troy has been reduced to rubble, long after Helen has been carted back to Lacedaemon, long after Agamemnon has met his sorry end, long after your own spirit has fled to the gloom of Tartarus – the poet Homer will record all of your travails in stunning verse. Nothing will be lost – not the endless sacrifices; not the compromises and petty foibles of the generals; not the sounds and sights of spilling gore or the dying cries of homesick boys; not the vindictive, implacable rage of Achilles; not the terrible, eternal grief of Hector's family. And not, definitely not, the whims and meddling and treachery of the capricious gods.

Soldiers on both sides have every reason to fear the gods, but no amount of pious abjection can guarantee their protection or dependability. You might imagine that you are being looked after, but you have no real way of being sure until a bronze-tipped spear miraculously glances off your breastplate or, conversely, plunges lethally into your bowels. Then you know; but even if you're spared this time, surviving once does not automatically mean you will survive again. It's all up to the gods, which is a little like placing your life in the hands of a class of cliquish schoolchildren.

Since every little reversal of fortune is the result of divine intervention, it's hardly surprising that everyone is a little confused as to when and why the gods are on their side or have abandoned them. You've heard Menelaus say, "When you fight a man against the will of the gods, a man they have sworn to honor – then look out." He's right, but the problem is, you can never know whom the gods have sworn to honor or whether they will abide by their word. Time and again, they descend to earth, assume human form, and whisper advice and blandishments into human ears. How to know who is who or whether you are getting good advice or bad? Any military historian will tell you that a battlefield is the worst place in the world for getting a sense of the big picture.

Look at the great heroes, the ones to whom the gods appear and make their will known. Even the generals are more or less clueless. There is no hotline to Olympus, and a man may be god-fearing all his life to no avail when push comes to shove. Zeus has a number of offspring on the battlefield, but they can't count on his protection. He even allows his own son Sarpedon to be slaughtered, specifically to discourage the other gods from playing favorites. Aeneas, Zeus's Trojan grandson, is spurred on to fight by the feckless Apollo, who promptly abandons him on the battlefield. It is Poseidon, a sworn enemy of Troy, who has to save him at the last minute. And why? "He always gave us gifts to warm our hearts, gifts for the gods who hold the vaulting skies." But then again, so does everyone else. Hector certainly did, as Zeus is compelled to admit: "He never stinted with gifts to please my heart. Never once did my altar lack its share of victims." Much good this did poor Hector when he needed help, as Apollo points out: "Now you cannot bring yourself to save him – even his corpse." Apollo is not much better, however. Supposedly the great protector of Troy, he simply throws in the towel and walks away from all his obligations in mid-battle. "Let these mortals fight themselves to death," he mutters, abandoning an entire city of devoted followers to a hideous fate. A god's allegiance is never bankable, no matter how much you've paid for it.

If a god breathes courage into one man, how can his opponent fail to blench like a coward? If a god strikes quaking fear into an entire army, what is the value of courage? If you are fated to die, why bother running? If you are slated for victory, whom should you fear? Do these gods to whom you relentlessly pray and sacrifice actually have the power to alter your destiny, or are they only playacting? To the soldier in the field, unable to conceive of a universe without moral cause and effect, it must have been maddeningly confusing.

From a modern perspective, we have to wonder why the Greeks bothered. Being in the thrall of their gods seems infinitely more dangerous, far less predictable and cost-effective than living in a genuinely random, material, and affectless universe. Such a universe was, of course, as unimaginable to them as theirs is to us. The overriding sense among the ancient Greeks seems to have been that, as bad as things could get, they could only be worse without divine sanction. It is better to know what you fear than to live in fear of the unknown. This point of view makes a little more sense off the battlefield, where strangers meet not in conflict, but in the sanctuary of hospitality.

"What are they here – violent, savage, lawless? Or friendly to strangers, god-fearing men?" On his arduous ten-year voyage home from Ilium, Odysseus is forced to ask himself this question again and again as he is cast up on one foreign shore after another, dependent on the kindness of strangers. What he really means is "Are these barbarians or Greeks?" Greeks know that the gods walk the earth in many guises and that any stranger who appears at your door could be a divine being testing your piety. So devotion begins at home, laid down in the rules of hospitality.

And the justly famous hospitality of ancient Greeks, especially as extended to strangers, is clearly linked to their deepest religious and cultural identity. Barbarians – even those who, like Polyphemus the Cyclops, enjoy divine ancestry – have no fear of the Greek gods and are therefore not bound by those rules. They are more likely to eat you. Equally liberated, you are now free to steal their cheese and to blind them with hot pokers.

Odysseus has any number of opportunities to sample the hospitality of strangers, good and bad, but never to question the assumption that the handles "god-fearing" and "friendly to strangers" are essentially synonymous. It is a simple equation: If you are afraid of the gods – and Odysseus, having sampled the measure of their temper in Troy, most certainly is – then you will be friendly to strangers. And since Zeus himself, as even the lowly pig herder Eumaeus knows, is the god of guests, you'd better get it right. If you don't, you could easily end up like any one of the poor fools who unwittingly offended the goddess Demeter's sense of good hospitality: Asclabus, turned into a gecko; King Lynkus, turned into a lynx; Colontas, burned to a crisp in his own house.

So a Greek knew what to expect from another Greek, friend or stranger, when he arrived at his home, and he knew why he could expect it: fear, pure and simple. Eumaeus makes it very clear to Odysseus, who has arrived home on Ithaca disguised as a beggar, why he is treating him so kindly. It is not because of the charming stories with which Odysseus regales him through the dark night: "Never for that will I respect you, treat you kindly; no, it's my fear of Zeus, the god of guests." Even Penelope's vicious suitors, who for years have abused her hospitality by camping out in her atrium, eating all her food and drinking her best wine, know why it is wrong for Antinous to strike a lowly beggar at the threshold: "Your fate is sealed if he's some god from the blue."

Their understanding of the rules of hospitality does not stop them from violating every single one, but it should, as they will soon find out to their chagrin.

Greek hospitality followed certain standard rituals that varied only in the luxury with which the host could afford to extend them. Visitors are warmly welcomed at the threshold and ushered in. "Greetings, stranger!" Telemachus hails Athene, disguised as a chieftain. "Here in our house you'll find a royal welcome. Have supper first, then tell us what you need." In a wealthy household, he – always he, as women do not travel alone or eat with the men – may first be led to the baths, where maidservants will wash him, anoint him with oil, and bring him fresh clothing. He will then be led to a comfortable chair. A servant brings a pitcher of water and a bowl with which the guest washes his hands. The housekeeper sets up a small table of food, usually simple bread and roast meats, along with a goblet of wine. The meat may be supplemented with a relish of raw onion, and a rich host may offer aged wine, into which he may grate goat cheese and sprinkle white barley, but there is no need whatsoever for luxury. The point is to refresh a weary traveler. It is only when the guest has put aside the desire for food and drink that the host is allowed to question him as intrusively as he will on his identity, his home, his family, and the purpose of his journey. It is at this point that guests arriving in disguise – gods masquerading as mortals or noblemen testing the probity of would-be allies – tend to reveal themselves. The talking goes on late, prolonged by lengthy genealogies and detailed accounts of every adventure, after which the honored guest will be led out to sleep under the shelter of the porch on a makeshift bed of throw rugs, blankets, and woolen robes.

At some point during the visit, some sort of offering will have to be made to the gods in thanksgiving or in hopes of a safe journey ahead. The offering may be as simple as a quick libation of wine poured into the ground or the singeing of the hair of the animal to be eaten. At the reconciliation of Achilles and Agamemnon, the butcher-priest Talthybius swings the sacrificial boar over his head like a shot put and flings it into the sea. When Nestor speeds Telemachus on his way, he propitiates Athene with a lavish sacrifice. The women sing sacred hymns while barley is scattered and hands are washed. The heifer's horns are clad in gold before she is cut down, her throat slit, her blood collected, her flesh and fat butchered, elaborately rearranged on wooden billets and burned, and her intestines sampled by the participants. Only then can her meat be spitted and roasted for consumption. Athene happens to be present for this particular sacrifice because Telemachus is her pet cause of the moment, and she may be presumed to be delighted, as she often is in her girlish way, by all the fuss.

When all goes well, when all the rules of hospitality are faithfully observed, the gods are satisfied, the traveler is sent safely on his way, and the wheels of the divine machine continue to spin smoothly and unhindered. Naturally enough, things can and do go wrong, with results that vary between the inconvenient and the cataclysmic. The Trojan war itself erupted as the result of a breach of these rules: Paris's abduction of Helen while his host was away at a funeral. Paris's misdeed was, of course, more than simply an example of a guest behaving badly, but it was explicitly recognized and condemned by Proteus as a crime against hospitality. The Cyclops episode, the slaughter of the Sun God's cattle and Circe's transformation of Odysseus' men into pigs are other cases in which a disregard for the obligations that guest and host owe one another is a direct cause of the ensuing debacle. Aeolus welcomes Odysseus to his island with a month of lavish feasting and all due honor, then sends him on his way with the gift of an ox-hide bag filled with howling winds. But when Odysseus' resentful sailors open the bag and their ship is blown all the way back to Aeolia, Aeolus is rightly convinced that his hospitality has been abused: "Away from my island – fast – most cursed man alive! It's a crime to host a man or speed him on his way when the blessed deathless gods despise him so. Crawling back like this – it proves the immortals hate you! Out – get out!" One of the most savage epithets that Medea can think of to hurl at Jason in her fury is that of "guest-deceiver."

Hardly a single disaster or peril is described in the vast annals of Greek mythology that is not, in some way, connected to the desecration of hospitality. Consider Psyche, who dares not accept the hospitality of Pluto on her journey to the underworld. Consider Phineus, on whom Zeus visits the plague of the Harpies, which swoop down upon his dinner table at every meal, steal his food, and leave nothing but stinking remnants, making it somewhat awkward for him to receive and entertain guests. Consider the hapless god Atlas, turned to stone for refusing hospitality to Perseus. Consider the bandit Procrustes, whose specialty was to offer a comfy bed to passersby, only to cut off their legs or stretch them on the rack in order to make them fit.

First and foremost, consider with dread – as did any Greek who ever contemplated abusing his guests in any way – the saga of Tantalus and his descendents. Of vast wealth and king of Lydia, Tantalus was much favored by the gods because Zeus was his father; he is said to have been the only mortal ever allowed a taste of ambrosia. For reasons that you probably had to be there to appreciate, Tantalus chose to put his patrons to the test by inviting them to a banquet at which he served up his own son Pelops, slaughtered, butchered, and boiled. His deception was discovered, but not before Demeter had helped herself to a tender joint. Pelops was restored to life with an ivory shoulder to replace the one that had been eaten, but Tantalus endures his torment in

Tartarus to this very day. Standing up to his chin in a lake of clear, fresh water under a tree groaning with ripe fruit of all kinds, he is wracked by hunger and thirst, but the waters recede whenever he bends to drink and the branches of the tree rise in the breeze, just out of reach whenever he stretches to eat.

His daughter Niobe, imperious queen of Thebes, lost all her children to the arrows of Apollo and Artemis and was eventually turned into a stone that is said to weep night and day. Pelops prospered, however, producing two strapping sons, Atreus and Thyestes, who cruelly vied with one another for the throne of Mycenae. Having temporarily achieved the upper hand, Atreus invited his brother to a lavish dinner at which, with a shameful lack of originality, he served up several of his nephews, Thyestes' sons, butchered and boiled according to an old family recipe. Sadly for Atreus, he failed to cook Thyestes' remaining son, Aegisthus, who eventually murdered him and restored his father to the throne.

Atreus had two sons, Agamemnon and Menelaus. Agamemnon eventually overthrew Thyestes, while Menelaus became king of Sparta. But in order to catch a favorable wind to Troy, Agamemnon agreed to sacrifice his daughter Iphigenia, for which his wife, Clytemnestra, was never quite able to forgive him. While he was away at war, she took his cousin Aegisthus for her lover; ten years later, upon the destruction of Troy, Aegisthus threw Agamemnon a spectacular homecoming banquet at which he slew him and all his men. Aegisthus was eventually killed by his nephew Orestes.

Five generations of bitter vendetta, all set in motion by an ill-considered menu.

Over the ensuing centuries, the Greeks slowly emerged from the darkness, recovering their literacy, developing city-states and leaving their tribal past behind. They planted colonies through-out the Mediterranean, Anatolia, and the Black Sea, founded a vast, if short-lived, empire, and came into contact with myriad diverse and far-flung peoples. This had the double benefit of enriching their civilization in countless ways while confirming their deep-rooted sense of superiority. Particularly after routing the Persians at the battles of Marathon, Salamis, and Plataea between 490 and 478 B.C., the Greeks of the classical age experi-enced the kind of blossoming of culture, wealth, and sophistica-tion from which heroic societies rarely recover.

In the sciences of gastronomy and the arts of hospitality, the peace dividend paid off handsomely and immediately. Suddenly, almost overnight in historical terms, we see an explosion of cookbook writing, especially in the wealthy Greek colonies and cities of southern Italy and Sicily, which developed such inter-national reputations for their decadent opulence that, to this very day, being a sybarite means more than simply being from the Calabrian town of Sybaris. Such Sicilian food writers as Matro of Pitane, Mithaikos, Heracleides and Agis of Syracuse were famous in their day. The greatest of them all, Archestratos of Gela, "Daedalus of tasty dishes" and author of *The Life of Luxury*, is said to have "circumnavigated the inhabited world for the sake of his belly and the portions of his anatomy below the belly" and to have been worshipped like Homer. His book, a kind of culinary travelogue, insists that we buy bread only from Lydian or Phoe-nician bakers, but disdains anyone who prefers Phoenician wine over Lydian as an *alazonochaunophluaron* – roughly, according to his translator, an "emptyheadedbrainlessbullshitartist." In *Deip-nosophistae*, his fifteen-book treatise on food and foodways, Athe-naeus of Naucratis is able to list at least eighteen cookbooks containing recipes for the spiced gravy known as *karyke*. A lost masterpiece, *The Art of Grocery Shopping* by Lynkeus of Samos, included advice on how to disparage fish by claiming them to be out of season, thus driving away customers and driving down prices.

A new profession was born: freelance catering. Professional caterers imported from Italy and Chios were all the rage, while hired cooks became stock figures in Greek comedy, like lawyers today. The wealthy found new ways of pampering themselves. According to Chamaeleon of Pontus, Smindyrides of Sybaris brought one thousand slaves – including fishermen, fowlers, and cooks – to his wedding to Agaristê, the daughter of Cleisthenes.

The Greeks – whom Athenaeus chides as "dinner-chasing Sophists" – began to sound suspiciously like New Yorkers. They yearned for simplicity yet craved the latest exotic imports. One minute they were indulging in *anthosmias* (wine adulterated with seawater to enhance its bouquet), *garos* (a ubiquitous sauce made of fish fermented in clay jars for months), haggis, and "pease purée poured over eggs, oysters and scallops"; the next, they were praising the simple traditional preparations of the old country and bemoaning the ultrasophistication of the Italians, who ruined good fish "by covering it with cheese and sprinkling it with liquid vinegar and silphium-flavored broth." In the land of Sophocles, Euripides, and Sappho, it was no longer blasphemy to assert, as did Euphron, that "the cook and the poet are just alike: the art of each lies in his brain." Sparta, its martial valor an anachronism, became a laughing stock for its "black broth."

"As gastronomy advanced, it left the gods behind," says food historian Andrew Dalby. He is suggesting not that the Greeks were in danger of abandoning their gods and religion, but rather that, as they advanced in sophistication and assimilated foreign ways, the intimate connection between food, hospitality, and piety became ever more ritualized, alienated from its origins as a genuine response to genuine terror before the unknown.

Nowhere is this evolution more evident than in the great symposia of Plato, Xenophon, and, later, Plutarch. Although such works spare no more than a passing mention of the food and drink served at these parties (which were distinct from and always followed dinner), none contains more than a glancing nod to piety, either. "They made libation and sang a chant to the god and so forth" is a fairly typical dismissal of the obligatory ritual.

The conversation at these parties was all directed to contemporary philosophical topics – democracy, individual freedom, logic, education, governance, nature, virtue, morality, love. The atmosphere was informal, playful, amicably competitive, rarely scholarly, often lubricious, and occasionally drunken. Friends reclined, two or three to a couch, drank, played parlor games, discussed the issues and personalities of the day, and made fun of each other and themselves. Socrates, fat, bald, and ugly, threatens to dance at Callias' symposium. Were it not for the entertainment – flute players, dancers, buffoons, prostitutes – and the scarcity of women, these parties could easily be taking place among well-educated urbanites in any modern capital. At least, since all the most learned and distinguished men of Athens were gathered in one *andron*, it is easy to imagine that the other, less high-minded symposia going on around town were devoted to the kind of talk we know so well – careers, sports, salacious gossip, real estate. These were not people who were afraid of being turned into geckos.

The participants in Plato's *Symposium* gather at the home of their friend Agathon to engage in a contest to deliver the best discourse on love. They are serious enough about the issue to agree to limit their drinking, an unusual enough occurrence in its own right, but are otherwise in a typically lighthearted, dinner-party frame of mind. Phaedrus begins by asserting that Love is among the oldest of the gods and makes men behave nobly and honourably because they would be ashamed of doing otherwise before their beloved. He even suggests that, for this reason, soldiers should go into battle with their (male) lovers, an idea which the Spartans had already put into practice. Pausanius, contrarily, reminds the symposiasts that Aphrodite, the goddess of love, has two natures: one that inspires noble love and virtue, including the love of friends and little boys whom one seeks to improve, and another that inspires the meaner, common forms of love, including the love of women. Eryximachus, a doctor, makes the analogy that, just as healthy and unhealthy elements vie within the human body and throughout nature, creating a tension that it is the physician's task to understand and balance, so too it is the task of the pious man to distinguish between healthy love and unhealthy love and thus to effect a reconciliation between men and gods. Aristophanes proposes that there was once an androgynous third sex, composed of two beings fused together face to face, that was punished for its hubris by being cut in two, and that love is the obscurely understood impulse of these incomplete halves to rejoin and complete each other. Agathon moves the discussion away from the effects of love and toward its nature, which is of surpassing beauty and goodness and thus the cause of beauty and goodness everywhere.

The final, falsely reluctant speaker is Socrates, who offers that love is neither beautiful nor good, but rather an intermediate, a search for something only dimly glimpsed. A wise man, he says, has no need to seek wisdom; an ignorant man cannot perceive the need to do so. So, too, someone who is loved does not seek love, while someone who cannot love does not see the need for it. Thus, love is to be found somewhere in between, in a spiritual quest, "for the whole of the spiritual is between divine and mortal . . . interpreting and transporting human things to the gods and divine things to men." From that point, Socrates gradually builds a vision of love that rises above attraction to beauty, above desire, above yearning for that which it lacks, above mortality and parenthood toward "a certain single knowledge connected with a beauty which has yet to be told." Love is infinite and immutable:

> Beginning from obvious beauties he must for the sake of that highest beauty be ever climbing aloft, as on the rungs of the ladder, from one to two, and from two to all beautiful bodies; from personal beauty he proceeds to beautiful observances, from observance to beautiful learning, and from learning at last to that particular study which is concerned with the beautiful itself and that alone.

At this point, the symposium is interrupted by the arrival of the drunken Alcibiades, who proceeds to offer a shameless account of his frustrated efforts to seduce Socrates and an encomium to the philosopher's endurance, courage, and wisdom. The party breaks up shortly afterward upon the invasion of a horde of drunken gate-crashers.

It is conceivable, I suppose, that not all readers will recognize their own party chatter in my synopsis of the *Symposium*. We do not, it is true, all discuss the spiritual nature of love at our dinner parties, drawing heavily on classical references, although we might. It is also possible, since Plato makes no claim to having been present at this particular symposium, that for literary purposes he has edited out the intervals in which the party-goers talked about their health problems, the cost of their children's schooling, street crime, and travel plans. What we do recognize – despite the absence of women and all the talk of sex with little boys – is the atmosphere in which people of a certain education and leisure, of all professions and from all walks of life, sit around of an evening to eat, drink, and exchange often ill-informed opinions in a spirit of friendly, casual companionship. That is us, and it is not Homer. We do not – at least, my friends and I do not – sit around worrying that God will punish us for our transgressions, and neither do Plato's or Xenophon's symposiasts. They, like us, have spent many centuries evaluating the evidence. Even if, like humans everywhere and at all times, they rarely have the fortitude of their convictions, they, like us, seem to have come to the conclusion that loving, forthright, and virtuous behavior toward their fellow men and women is rewarded, materially and spiritually, far better than abjection and the slavish placation of occult forces. Violent, slave-owning misogynists they may yet be, but just look at the quagmire of fear and ignorance from which they have had to extricate themselves. I am almost tempted to say that they – and by implication, we – have evolved. A little.

As with us, however, this evolution has been incremental and not fully iconoclastic. Just as it is impossible to understand the ideas and morals of the twenty-first century without harking back at least to the sixteenth, so with the Greeks of Plato's time it is probably just as important to examine what they have chosen to preserve from their ancestry as it is to evaluate what they have jettisoned. We retain our mythologies, archaic as well as contemporary, because they remain pertinent by telling us something about ourselves. Ancient stories, such as those related by Ovid in his *Metamorphoses*, can reveal the continuity of ideas and attitudes even as they evolve beyond recognition.

Ovid relates how Theseus and his companions, on their way to Athens, are waylaid by the river god Achelous, who is anxious to extend his hospitality to the great hero. While they are waited upon by barefoot nymphs, Achelous tells them the story of how Neptune turned the maiden Perimele into an island. When

Pirithous, one of Theseus' company, expresses scornful scepticism about the truth of the story, the aged hero Lelex sets him straight.

He recounts the tale of Baucis and Philemon, a pious old couple living in the hill country of Phrygia. One day, they take in a pair of footsore travelers who had been turned away from every other home in the region. Though poor and living without servants in a tiny thatched cottage, the hosts seek to make their guests comfortable in every way. Baucis seats them on sedge-grass mattresses, which she covers with her best cloth, and engages them in chitchat to distract them from the wait for their humble meal. She props up the leg of a rickety table, which she wipes clean with green mint. The travelers are given a homey meal of cheese, olives, garden vegetables, boiled bacon, roasted eggs, and young wine served in beechwood cups coated in yellow wax – just about everything the household has to offer. They enjoy a dessert of figs, dates, honeycomb, and grapes fresh off the vine.

As the meal progresses, the hosts notice that the flagon of wine keeps refilling itself. Their guests, it transpires, are the gods Zeus and Hermes (Ovid uses their Roman names) touring the country in disguise. The old couple, ashamed by the scantiness of the meal, want to sacrifice their one goose, but the bird eludes them and is finally offered protection by the gods.

Baucis and Philemon are led to a hilltop, whence they witness the flooding of the entire countryside in punishment for its wicked lack of hospitality. Only their thatched cottage is spared, transformed into a gleaming temple of gold and marble. Offered any reward for their piety, the couple ask only to be allowed to serve as priests in the temple and, at their appointed time, to die together so that neither might have to live alone. All this is granted and, on the day of their deaths many years later, they have just enough time to whisper a hasty good-bye before being transformed into trees, an oak and a linden, that flourish side by side for centuries thereafter.

Although they never knew it, Baucis and Philemon have waited their entire lives for this divine encounter. All the stories on their parents' knees, all the religious training, all the practice and patience of hospitality have led up to their meeting with the gods. They have won the lottery: millions upon millions of Greek hosts, every bit as humble and diligent as they, lived and died anonymously without ever being put to the test. By all lights, Baucis and Philemon should be trembling in their sandals, paralyzed with dread as they face their moment of truth. How many thousands have come to this crossroads and failed to pass through, being transformed for their sins into birds, beasts, inanimate objects, geographical features, or the tortured damned?

But Baucis and Philemon are serene and unafraid, evincing but a momentary alarm when they first come to understand the situation. In fact, the entire story, despite the destruction, is suffused with a most gentle and transcendent love that transmutes all it touches. The love of supplicants for their masters, which, like a child's love for his or her parents, is trusting and never abstract; the protective, sheltering, divine love in which the righteous bask so peacefully, like thoughtless lizards in the desert; the love of the host for order, calm, and cleanliness, all enwrapped in a sprig of green mint; the love of the gardener for nature's simple bounty; most of all, an old couple's love for each other, as elemental and encompassing and eternal as the Earth itself, a sanctuary as holy and sanctifying as any temple, as deep-rooted and phototropic as any linden tree. With barely a pittance of learning between them, Baucis and Philemon live in full conceit of the love that Plato is at such pains to transpose.

Socrates, Plato, and their peers were fully aware that they were not the same as the Greeks of Achilles' time, or of Homer's time, or of Baucis and Philemon's time, and they congratulated themselves on it. What they were probably less attuned to were the ways in which they were similar and, in some respects, the ways in which they fell short in understanding.

It is entirely plausible, in fact, that, having put such an enormous distance between themselves and their god-fearing ancestors, the philosophers and intellectuals of Plato's time had, all unwittingly, lost something of great value and beauty. They may well have seen Homer's characters as fearful, superstitious barbarians, not unlike our view of them, timeless poetry notwithstanding. Perhaps, though, what the Homeric Greeks were really afraid of was not the wrath of the gods, but that the gods might not exist after all. Perhaps they peopled the universe with gods not to explain and propitiate the unknown, but to serve as epitomes for their own inchoate need to aspire, to love transcendentally – in other words, as instinctual expressions of the very same love that Socrates explicates at great length. If that is the case – if Homer understood this love just as deeply and transcendently as Socrates – it turns our theory of ancient Greek hospitality as god-fearing placation on its head. In humble hospitality, we do not placate the gods, but *create* them.

This brings us full circle to the paralysis of fear I sometimes experience before the arrival of my guests. If, in welcoming people into my home, what I am actually doing is summoning the presence of the divinity, is it any wonder that I tremble before the prospect of this unfolding miracle? Just as Plato describes, we long; in longing, we look around ourselves for the object of our longing, and, not finding it, we look upward. If we do not find it there, there is nowhere left to turn but to the Baucis or Philemon beside us. What is real is our love; what is contingent is its object. So what if, in its contingency, that object is also an object of dread? That stranger at your threshold, that friend across the table: is she a god to be feared or is she that "certain single knowledge" of yours, your love which has yet to be told, embodied and emboldened to seek your welcome, to come home to you and your hospitality – transfigured, like a tumbledown cottage of Phrygia, into a Temple of Love.

After all, when we lie awake in bed late at night, or as we prepare to receive the guests whom we have summoned to the table, in Phrygia as in Manhattan, what is it that pains us the most: our terror, or our longing?

CHAPTER IX

THANKSGIVING, NEW YORK CITY, 2001

*They dwelt in ease and peace upon their lands with many good things,
rich in flocks and loved by the blessed gods.*

Hesiod, *Works and Days*

The calendar tells us that Thanksgiving falls on the last Thursday of November, but that is only partly true. We may celebrate it on that date, but it can no more be confined to a single day than love can be confined to Valentine's Day. Thanksgiving is the commemoration – the act of remembering together – of an event, but I would imagine that few, if any of us are thinking about pilgrims and Indians as the day dawns. We come together and we remember something altogether different. Those memories that impose themselves on us on Thanksgiving Day are our own, with us at all times, guardian angels and devil provocateurs that never sleep but do not always speak to us directly. Instead, they hold their tongues until we come together to commemorate, and then those memories talk to each other in their own ancient language, like a group of dogs on a walk, straining at the leash, sniffing at each other, circling warily. We see them come alive then, among their own, but, like the owners of those dogs, we have no idea what they are saying to each other. We only think we own them. And even when we get them home, alone together on the couch, and we scratch them between the ears and offer them tidbits, those memories still can't tell us what they want from us.

On Wednesday, I get up before dawn to buy Brussels sprouts, potatoes, yams, lettuce, and herbs at the farmers market on Union Square. I drop these off at home and then head directly for Jefferson Market, where I pick up the twenty-five pound organic turkey that I had ordered several weeks earlier. I've learned from experience that a twenty-five pounder is the largest that will fit in my lobster pot, where it will soak in brine and herbs for the next twenty-four hours. If I have timed everything right, I should have about half an hour left before work to make a last quick excursion to the supermarket for butter, half-and-half, and cream. By the time I get home from work that evening, I'm already wiped out. We husband our energies, kick back in front of the television, drink iced vodka, and order in.

Thursday morning, the entire household is mobilized. There are sprouts, potatoes, onions, carrots, parsnips, and chestnuts to be peeled. There is sausage to be fried and fresh sage, rosemary, tarragon, oregano, and thyme to be chopped. The stuffing has to be mixed. There are mashed potatoes with crème fraîche, root vegetables roasted with sesame oil, Brussels sprouts sautéed with chestnuts and ham, creamed pearl onions, gravy, cranberry relish, salad, and dressing to be prepared. The turkey must be drained, washed, dried, seasoned, stuffed, slathered with herb butter inside and out, mounted, and in the oven by nine o'clock. Then there are glasses to dust, napkins to be ironed, floors to be mopped, children to be groomed, and a hamster cage to be disinfected. At noon we rest; at two the guests begin to arrive.

The mood is thoughtful and emotional as our guests assemble. My father is already here, as are my sisters, Nancy and Jenny, visiting from England. Of my immediate family, only my brother

Scott, tied up in L.A. on a film shoot, along with his wife, Adena, and their children, Seth and Michaela, are missing. Judy's parents arrive first, her mother, Herzlia, bearing pumpkin scones, her father, David, with some very special Burgundy that he and I will share only reluctantly with the others. Then come Judy's sister, Barbara, and her new husband, Andy. My father's first cousin Norman and his wife, Irene, arrive, bringing cranberry mold and cranberry sauce; then their daughter, Maggi, on whom I had a secret crush as a teenager, with her husband, Michael, their girls, Sarah and Kate, and pumpkin pie. Then comes Jennifer, Maggi's sister, with her husband, Larry, their children, Max and Harry, and chocolate mousse cake. We welcome my father's friends Billy, who has brought two enormous platters of steamed shrimp, and Bernice, a colleague of thirty years. Our old friend Margaret has driven down from Wellesley with her two-year-old, Ben. There are only twenty-five of us this year; we have numbered as many as thirty at Thanksgivings past.

Some years, Thanksgiving is the only chance I get to see my cousins, although they only live across town. Every year, we have to remind the children how they are related: Norman and Irene are my first cousins once removed; Maggi and Jennifer are my second cousins; Sarah, Kate, Max, and Harry are my second cousins once removed, and Sophie's and Cora's third cousins. This is a puzzle they love to solve, the same game that had delighted me twenty-five years earlier at our Thanksgivings in London and filled me, harboring my illicit passion for Maggi, with the ancient thrill of violated taboo. When they are finally satisfied with the exegesis of the family tree, the children go off to play Twister and listen to Destiny's Child.

All the prep work is done and I can relax. We eat shrimp, drink scotch or chardonnay. Naturally, all the talk is about the World Trade Center attack. Many of us had witnessed it as it happened;

Andy had had to scramble down thirty-eight flights of stairs from his office in WTC 7, which collapsed later in the day; he had arrived at our door covered in a thin film of white dust. None of us, New Yorkers all, had lived a moment since then without reliving the horrors of that day. Even now, some ten weeks later, our windows are tightly shut against the burning stench that continues to rise from the crater less than two miles due south.

Twilight falls early in New York in late November, and it has already begun when the turkey comes out of the oven. It rests, as massive and still as a monument, while Norman retrieves his freshly laundered apron, carving knife, and fork from his brief-case. Norman has been honorary carver for as long as I can recall, and I don't believe that even he remembers when or why he started bringing his own implements. He takes his time sharpening the blade, as he knows that it is not really right to launch the feast until it is dark outside, for that is when the lights are dimmed, the candles lit, and the apartment begins to feel en-closed and aglow from within, as it were, like a stage in a darkened theater. No feast or drama can be entirely successful until this sense of isolation from the outside world is complete and an entirely artificial and hermetic universe has been created. That is how the trance of hospitality is summoned; that is how we close our eyes, descend into the deep, and retrieve by sense of touch the remembrance of long-gone celebration. When the lights are low and the autumn night closes in, the host's most important task of all – that of marrying the dream of the present to the dream of the past – may begin.

The actual Thanksgiving meal is the least important element of the celebration, for me at any rate. For one thing, there are too many of us to sit in one gathering at the table, so the eternal, circular aspect of the banquet – normally so crucial to any prospect of a successful dinner – has to be discarded. Instead, we have several tables set up, and people rise and move around as the whim takes them; naturally, in these circumstances, they are less inclined to linger approvingly over their food. For another, as fresh, bountiful, and all-American as it is, there is more bulk than elegance to the fare. The diners – who are serving themselves, buffet-style – tend to overload their plates and shovel down their food with a lack of appreciation and decorum that might demolish a fastidious cook in other circumstances. They are going straight for *ataraxia*, without any of the intervening stages of pleasure. There are, of course, the usual comments on the juiciness of the bird, the hint of armagnac in the gravy, the creaminess of the potatoes, but my guests have been eating this food for years and are not looking for surprises. The chef cannot and should not hope for the praise and wide-eyed wonder that his cooking usually elicits. I, for one, always lose interest if I cannot expect to be praised.

So the entire meal is wiped out in an hour or less. The wine, the somnolence of satiety, and the prospect of several hours of cleanup keep us all glued to our seats. I do not get to see my sisters nearly as often as I would like, and we retire to a quiet corner with my father for a chat. Tonight, we are feeling particularly thankful and especially giving. We cannot continue to talk or think any longer about September 11; it is time to forget for a while.

My father begins to reminisce about the Thanksgivings of his childhood. He grew up in the Bronx during the Depression, not poor but in very modest circumstances. An only child, he slept on a daybed in the front vestibule, a latchkey kid who spent a lot of time on his own. My grandfather worked collecting insurance premiums door to door; my grandmother clerked at a department store. Along with steaks and chops, she had a deft hand with traditional Eastern European fare – borscht, schav, mamaliga, schmaltz herring. She made her own caviar out of whitefish roe, grated onion, olive oil, and lemon juice. In the hot summers, they ate cucumber salad and calves' foot jelly. Within their means, they enjoyed entertaining; an expandable bridge table was set up in the living room for big events. My father always looked forward to the company.

But the great event of the year was the gathering of the Browner clan at Thanksgiving, at Uncle Dick and Aunt Rose's house. Uncle Dick, whose real name was Isidore, was the family success story – a traffic court judge. For a kid from the Bronx, a visit to Dick and Rose's colonial home in the leafy suburb of Great Neck was like a vacation to an exotic foreign country – or, more accurately, to the all-American dream that my father otherwise knew only from the movies. There was a lawn, with trees. The children had their own rooms. There was a dining room, and a buzzer under the rug at the head of the table for signaling staff in the kitchen.

Best of all, for my father, there were people – a press of aunts, uncles, grandparents, cousins of all ages. This was what family life was like in the movies, too: children running up and down the carpeted stairway or congregating in secret conclaves behind the garage; my grandfather and his brothers – Ben, Harry, Dick, and Max "the Irishman," a fireman – gathered around the blazing hearth with their drinks; the women in the kitchen, exchanging recipes and gossip. Who cared that Rose was an indifferent cook who got her cranberry sauce from a can? So what if there was no "staff" to respond to her buzzer? So what if everyone secretly scorned Dick as a blowhard and a bully? For my father, it was still as good as it gets: a crowd, a house, a meal, a happy noise. He recalls waking up in his father's arms late one Thanksgiving night as they walked through the cold, clean air of Great Neck to the railroad station, the crunch of snow underfoot mingling with the soothing wail of a distant fire engine.

My father had drawn on all these memories when, early in their married life, he and my mother began to host Thanksgivings of their own. It was not the menu he sought to re-create, nor the guest list, but the sense memory and the feelings of safety and wholeness, so fleeting yet so overwhelming in childhood, and so rarely recaptured since. Maybe it never even existed, that feeling, but we insist that it did because we cannot give up the fetish we have made of taking out and polishing its memory on special days. The feeling itself we chase throughout our adult lives, as we might a false image burned into our retinas of an object that has long since vanished and did not in any case resemble the picture we retained of it.

Prompted by my father, my sisters and I indulge in our own maudlin reminiscence. It takes us back a quarter of a century, to London, 1976. Night falls even earlier there than it does in New York; it is stiller and darker yet. Our dining room, its walls hunter green, its floor carpeted in blue-and-green tartan, has a calming, quieting effect on all who enter. Its one enormous window frames the spotlit tower of Westminster Cathedral. The walls are hung with vintage and contemporary posters. The table is a large hunter's trestle, set with blue Italian pottery and French restaurant flatware in the same pattern that Judy and I would choose for ourselves twenty years later. The food is ready on a marble-topped sideboard: turkey, stuffing, potatoes mashed and roasted, Brussels sprouts, creamed onions, cranberry sauce. The soundtrack to *A Chorus Line* plays softly in the background.

Some of the same people are here, too: My father, we children, Norman, Irene, Maggi, and Jennifer. There are close family friends and several young American expatriates, alone and lonely in a foreign city, whom we have adopted for the evening. Only my mother is missing. She is sick, deeply debilitated by an aggressive strain of multiple sclerosis. For almost two years now, she has lived in a nursing home.

From the vantage of our corner of a New York City loft in 2001, we watch them all. Is it they, forever reenacting their gay, oblivious ritual, or is it we, melancholy, disembodied observers, who are the ghosts? They are much younger than we are; more carefree, perhaps. They do not know what we know; they are strange to us now. Scott is already tipsy on stolen sips of wine; he does not know that my father will make him go to school hungover tomorrow. Nancy is a distracted, coltish teenager; she does not know that she will soon meet the man with whom she will still be in love twenty-five years later. Jenny is a timid, love-hungry child, awed by and mistrustful of the unaccustomed serenity and harmony. My father is youthful and handsome, with a jaunty mustache and a full head of curly brown hair, proud of the distinguished brushstrokes of gray that have recently appeared at his temples. He is exactly as old as I am now.

Strangest and most distant of all, to me, is the skinny, fifteen-year-old boy in his National Health glasses and bell-bottoms that barely reach his ankles. His hair hangs almost to his shoulders and has not been brushed in many weeks. He is small, four inches shorter than he will be two years later, and uses the fact that he does not look his age to sly advantage. Like his brother, he sips surreptitiously at other people's drinks, but he is more careful; he reserves his serious drinking and antisocial misconduct for other occasions, since he knows how much more he can get away with by maintaining the façade of the sweet little boy. He watches Norman carve the turkey and asks earnest, well-informed questions. He tells cheeky, precocious jokes to the single adults. Understanding that the direct approach from someone as awkward and funny-looking as he is will never work with Maggi, a woman at sixteen, he sends her shy, puppyish glances on the unlikely chance that she will take pity on him. Unprovoked, he says cruel and nasty things to little Jenny when no one is watching.

Tonight, he is untouchable. He is ebullient, in his element. Everyone is here, everyone is together; this is a good family to be a member of on Thanksgiving. There are friends here, candles, music, comforting food, and sophisticated conversation. He is surrounded by merry, attractive adults who laugh knowingly at his jokes, who jostle him with affection, and who, he is sure, trade admiring anecdotes about him and predict his brilliant future as soon as he turns away. If he is good for nothing else, he knows how to perform for an audience. Most especially, he knows how to perform for his father, the wittiest, most sophisticated of them all. Everybody loves his father; tonight, they love the boy and his father can see that. There is safety and simplicity under his father's approving gaze. If the thought of his mother crosses his mind he doesn't acknowledge it, least of all to himself. This feeling – this confidence, this security, this togetherness – the boy wishes it could last forever, though he knows it won't. Tomorrow is not Thanksgiving.

Later on the night of Thanksgiving 2001, with guests long gone, the dishes washed and put away, and Judy asleep beside me, I lay in bed, exhausted but too overwrought to sleep. Nostalgia, of course, is as powerful a stimulant as pornography, and serves a similar purpose. This was not the first time I had so abused it; as a matter of fact, I had long been aware of the connection between certain unresolved childhood "issues" and my abiding need to serve and please. But tonight, with the help of my sisters and father, I had established the intimacy of that connection with stark and startling clarity. It seemed that I, like my father before me, was something of a tragic scientist: having once accidentally discovered the secret formula for perfect happiness, and then lost it, I had spent the rest of my days vainly trying to re-create the precise conditions of the original experiment. If you looked at it that way, it was perfectly clear that I could never, ever hope to succeed, since the missing ingredient was one that could not be reproduced. If I were Epicurus, I'd have probably figured out by now that I would be better off seeking to abolish the desire than to fulfill it. Inner turmoil and anxiety was all it had and all it would ever bring me; *ataraxia* was not in the cards.

With these and similarly uplifting thoughts, I eventually fell asleep. I awoke with a start in the middle of the night. I had been dreaming about Brussels sprouts. Again.

By the time my mother's illness took a turn for the worse in the early 1970s, my parents were already separated. My father lived in a series of little flats all over London, while we children stayed with our mother. Almost from the beginning she was physically unable to take care of us. Within three years, she lost first the ability to walk without a cane, then to walk without a walker, then to walk at all, and eventually even to rise from bed unassisted. I was barely able to remember what it was like to have a healthy mother, or the person she had been before the disease robbed her of her patience, good humor, and dignity.

We children were assisted in her care by a variety of woefully unqualified nannies, who often came with their own pressing emotional needs and demands. When we were not helping my mother to dress, bathe, eat, and use the toilet, we were largely left to our own devices. With the exception of little Jenny, who was too young to exercise any meaningful independence, we all took full advantage of our freedom, while doing our best to act responsibly toward our mother and to conceal the chaos of our household from our friends. That, at least, is how I remember it.

It must have been sometime in 1974 that my brother, sisters, and I were gathered for supper one evening around the Formica pedestal table in the kitchen. My mother had joined us, which by then she was not always in a condition to do. She was still capable of feeding herself at that point, but I imagine that one of us must have cut up her food for her. I do not remember what we ate that night, but it included Brussels sprouts, steamed or boiled whole. It was a relatively normal evening, unusual perhaps in that we were all eating together and speaking civilly. But then the talking stopped and we all turned to watch my mother.

She had raised a Brussels sprout to her mouth with a fork, but had neglected to spear it. This was a mistake, as her hands trembled badly at all times. Still, it looked as if she was going to make it, but at the last minute, the sprout, bobbling at the tip of the fork, bounced off and into her face. She managed to wedge it against her cheek with the ball of her thumb but was unable to grasp it. Her lips strained and twisted to the side in an effort to rendezvous with the sprout as she pushed it toward her mouth. Instead, the sprout rolled in the opposite direction, down the narrow channel between her cheek and her forearm. In order to keep the sprout within striking distance, she had to continually raise her arm as it rolled, until it had rolled down the entire length of her forearm and bicep and came to a halt near her armpit, in which she now buried her face to retrieve it. We watched, enthralled and horror-stricken. This was some sort of gladiatorial combat for her, a fight to the death; she had clearly invested her entire will in victory and, having come so far, would settle for nothing less. But it was not to be. A moment later, she and we watched helplessly as the Brussels sprout broke free, skittered down the front of her muumuu and disappeared in the gap between the cushion and the armrest of her wheelchair.

I don't know who started laughing first, but soon the four of us were purple-faced with suppressed snickering. My mother brushed a stray wisp of her mousy hair off her forehead and her eyes filled with tears. Here in England, three thousand miles from home, there was no one in the world who could stop her children from laughing at her infirmity. "It's not funny," she said in the half-whisper that had lately become her normal speaking voice. We knew only too well how not funny it was, maybe even more than she did, so we laughed harder. "It's not FUNNY!" she screamed, strangling on her outrage. She unlocked the brakes of her chair, wheeled around, and rolled from the room.

It must have been soon after this incident that the decision was made that she could no longer be looked after at home. I remember very little about those dark times, but her removal, and my father's immediate return home, surely came as a terrible relief and release. She entered the first of several nursing homes, each abysmal in its own way, and went into a steep decline. She suffered from bedsores and recurring pneumonia that left her febrile and incoherent for weeks on end. She was in her early forties, but she looked sixty. When she was able, she continued to smoke, inhaling through a long rubber tube attached to a cigarette holder soldered to the arm of her wheelchair. The chair was always parked bedside, but was now of little use, since her garret room was at the end of a long, dimly lit corridor at the top of a series of narrow, dog-legged stairways, and there was no elevator.

Although it was only a ten-minute walk from school, I found every excuse to avoid visiting her, and because Jenny was reliant on me, mostly, to take her there, they, too, saw little of one another. Once a week, for half an hour or forty-five minutes, was about all I could manage, but even that schedule was subject to the other priorities on my busy agenda. Sometimes I went two weeks without dropping in, and I counted myself lucky that I was allowed to get away with it.

She died of pneumonia on Monday, December 13, 1976 – two weeks after Thanksgiving. Marion Claire Browner.

I look back at those hallucinatory years, and I shake my head in amazement. I ask myself: Is it possible – is it even *conceivable* – that we had been celebrating our family togetherness on that Thanksgiving Day while she lay dying, alone and frightened? Had there really been all that laughter, and good food, and wine, and music, and tender feeling? From my dark bed in New York City, 2001, I take another look at those ghosts of 1976, and they look even more remote than before. Yes, there they all were, laughing and stuffing their faces. There had been no mistake. And there I was, baby-faced imposter, fawning for attention, ingratiating myself with all and sundry, hungry for love and praise. And eating Brussels sprouts.

And who am I – forty-year-old ghost of 2001, family man, father of two, Lord of Strangers – to judge those long-vanished revelers? Objectively, it is not all that difficult to understand, if not to justify, why I behaved the way I did. It is only natural, after all, to seek relief from one's troubles wherever one can find it, especially at the age of fifteen. I'm hardly in a position to deny that I would do exactly the same in similar circumstances. Is it so terrible, after all, that we honored the hospitality of Thanksgiving so intensely not in spite of my mother's imminent death, but because of it? Although it may feel to me now that one was committed, it is not a crime to celebrate life in the face of death. Surely, celebration trumps commemoration?

And yet, try as I might, I cannot entirely shake the feeling that, if their hospitality was based on a lie, then mine – which deliberately seeks to recall and revive it — must be too. Try as I might, I can't quite allay the suspicion that the authentic symbol of Thanksgiving is not a magnificent, twenty-five-pound turkey, brined, herbed, and roasted to golden perfection, but a humble

Brussels sprout, peeled of its tough outer leaves and steamed al dente. And I have grown to enjoy it more and more, in all its virtuous simplicity, with every passing year.

There is only so much bad news about himself that one person can absorb. He tires of it all, even when he knows it to be true. The truth is always exhausting, and cloying, which is why we tend to prefer it in small doses. We yearn to be let off the hook, to find religion, but the antidote to truth is not falsehood, any more than the antidote to overeating is vomiting. The antidote to truth is forgetfulness.

We live to forget: our lonely childhood, our idyllic childhood, our loneliness, our former happiness, our hunger, our humiliation at the hands of our own desires, our strangulating covetousness, our cruelties, our pathetic mortalities, our identities. With every step forward we build a wall between ourselves and the place we had stood a moment before. What wouldn't we choose to forget, given half the chance? Forgetfulness is a survival mechanism, as necessary as claws, as adrenaline, as the gag reflex. Whatever it is, it is not a moral issue. Where my father commemorates to remember, I commemorate to forget.

Of what good are our intellect, our passion, our reason, our compassion to us here? How few of us know what we want and, not knowing, are able to reach for it! And yet, useless as most of us are at succeeding in the least exercise of any importance – such as the pursuit of happiness – we have been very inventive in the myriad ways we have found to console ourselves. We can take pride in our achievements – art, religion, love, philosophy – when we are otherwise unable to express our simplest thought or desire.

And among these, our highest accomplishments, we cannot forget to rank hospitality. Hospitality provides one of the few settings in life where we can get exactly what we want from each other without having to ask for it. In other words, in which we can forget that we live in a world where this is otherwise, and tragically, entirely impossible.

When I am a good host, I can order the world precisely as I believe it ought to be. It is a world that I have created in my mind and in my own image, and it gladdens me profoundly to see it unfold without original sin, without expulsions and floods and disobedience and illness. When I am a good guest, I have returned to Eden, where everything I need is provided for me, including companionship and a benevolent deity at my shoulder, serving me *and* protecting me. The concept of paradise may be backward-looking, but the concept of heaven is anticipatory. Perhaps this is what heaven will be like? A great table of oak worn smooth with age and candle wax; a dimly lit room, a quartet of angels playing Sarah Vaughan in the corner; this blissful throb of quiet, intelligent conversation; bubbling pots and aromatic stews that no one seems to have worked to prepare; and you – you have nothing to worry about, not now, not here, not for all eternity. Leave it all behind at the threshold, forget everything, for here, in heaven, you are my guest.

ACKNOWLEDGMENTS

For her love, generosity, and patience, I thank Judy Clain first of all.

For their support and friendship, I also wish to thank Gail Hochman, Karen Rinaldi, and Gillian Blake; my father, Richard Browner, and siblings, Jenny, Nancy, and Scott Browner; my poker buddies Guy Yarden, Jim Browne, Eduardo Kaplan, Chris Skutch, Sam Sarowitz, and Eric Anderson; David Oestreicher; as well as Charlott Card, Hertzie Clain, Nick Clements, Edward Schneider, and Shelley Sonenberg.

I also thank Rebecca Saletan and Rick Kott for their invaluable advice early in this project.

BIBLIOGRAPHY

I am not a professional historian. I have tried, wherever possible, to stick to primary source material, which I have read with the eye of a novelist, seeking out character and story. Very little of this book's contents represents original research, and most of my sources will be familiar to anyone with a motivated interest in any particular subject. I have therefore prepared this bibliography in the spirit of offering a list of recommended further reading, rather than an academic resource.

Introduction

Brillat-Savarin, Jean-Anthelme. *The Physiology of Taste*. New York: Penguin, 1994.

Epicurus, *The Essential Epicurus: Letters, Principal Doctrines, Vatican Sayings, and Fragments*. Translated by Eugene Michael O'Connor. New York: Prometheus Books, 1993.

Chapter I

Bacque, James. *Crimes and Mercies: The Fate of German Civilians Under Allied Occupation, 1944–1950*. Toronto: Little, Brown, 1997.

Barkas, Janet. *The Vegetable Passion: A History of the Vegetarian State of Mind*. London: Routledge & Kegan Paul, 1975.

Bewley, Charles. *Hermann Göring and the Third Reich: A Bibliography Based on Family and Official Records*. New York: Devin-Adair, 1962.

Brupbacher-Bircher, Bertha. *Health-giving dishes, compiled by Bertha Brupbacher-Bircher, manageress of Dr. Bircher's sanatorium*. London: E. Arnold, 1934.

Butler, Ewan, and Gordon Young. *The Life and Death of Hermann Goering*. New York: David & Charles Pubs., 1989.

Goebbels, Joseph. *The Goebbels Diaries, 1939–1941*. Translated by Fred Taylor. London: H. Hamilton, 1982.

Goebbels, Joseph. *The Goebbels Diaries, 1942–43*. Translated by Louis P. Lochner. Garden City: Doubleday, 1948.

Gordon, Bertram M. "Fascism, the Neo-Right and Gastronomy." In the *Proceedings of the Oxford Symposium on Food & Cookery*. Devon, England: Prospect Books, 1987.

Gordon, Bertram M., and Lisa Jacobs-McCusker. "One Pot Cookery and Some Comments on Its Iconography." In the *Proceedings of the Oxford Symposium on Food & Cookery*. Devon, England: Prospect Books, 1988.

Göring, Emmy. *My Life with Goering*. London: David Bruce and Watson Ltd., 1972.

Infield, Glenn B. *Hitler's Secret Life: The Mysteries of the Eagle's Nest*. New York: Stein and Day, 1979.

Morell, Theo. *Adolf Hitler, the Medical Diaries: The Private Diaries of Dr. Theo Morell*. Edited by David Irving. London: Sidgwick & Jackson, 1983.

Mosley, Leonard. *The Reich Marshal: A Biography of Hermann Goering*. Garden City: Doubleday, 1974.

Schütz, W. W. *German Home Front*. London: V. Gollancz, 1943.

Steinhoff, Johannes et al. *Voices from the Third Reich: An Oral History*. Washington, D.C.: Regnery Gateway, 1989.

Speisenzusammenstellung unter Mitverwedung von Edelsoja Mit Kochanweisungen (Formulation of menus including pure soya, with recipes). Oberkommando der Werhmacht (Army High Command) Office of Foreign Agricultural Relations, USDA. Washington, D.C., 1941.

Toland, John. *Adolf Hitler*. Garden City: Doubleday, 1976.

Visser, Margaret. *The Rituals of Dinner: The Origins, Evolution, Eccentricities, and Meaning of Table Manners*. New York: Penguin, 1991.

Chapter II

Anderson, Sherwood. *Letters of Sherwood Anderson*. Boston: Little, Brown, 1953.

Darroch, Sandra Jabson. *Ottoline: The Life of Lady Ottoline Morrell*. New York: Coward, McCann & Geoghegan, 1975.

Flanner, Janet. *Paris Was Yesterday, 1925–1939*. Edited by Irving Drutman. New York: Viking, 1968.

Holroyd, Michael. *Lytton Strachey: A Biography*. New York: Penguin, 1980.

Huxley, Aldous. *Crome Yellow*. Chicago: Dalkey Archive, 2001.

Lawrence, D. H. *Women in Love*. New York: Doubleday, 1999.

McAlmon, Robert, and Kay Boyle. *Being Geniuses Together, 1920–1930*. San Francisco: North Point Press, 1984.

Mellow, James R. *Charmed Circle: Gertrude Stein & Co.* New York: Praeger, 1974.

Morrell, Ottoline. *Lady Ottoline's Album*. Edited by Carolyn G. Heilbrun. New York: Knopf, 1976.

Morrell, Ottoline. *Memoirs of Lady Ottoline Morrell*. Edited by Robert Gathorne-Hardy. New York: Knopf, 1964.

Morrell, Ottoline. *Ottoline at Garsington: Memoirs of Lady Ottoline Morrell, 1915–1918*. Edited by Robert Gathorne-Hardy. New York: Knopf, 1975.

Putnam, Samuel. *Paris Was Our Mistress*. New York: Viking, 1947.

Russell, Bertrand. *The Autobiography of Bertrand Russell, 1872–1914*. Vol. 1–3. London: George Allen and Unwin, 1967.

Sprigge, Elizabeth. *Gertrude Stein: Her Life and Work*. New York: Harper & Brothers, 1957.

Stein, Gertrude. *The Autobiography of Alice B. Toklas*. New York: Library of America, 1998.

Toklas, Alice B. *The Alice B. Toklas Cookbook*. New York: Anchor, 1954.

Chapter III

Audubon, John James. *Writings and Drawings*. New York: Library of America, Penguin Putnam, 1999.

Call, Richard Ellsworth. "The Life and Writings of Rafinesque." Paper prepared for the Filson Club and read at its meeting, Louisville, Ky., April 2, 1894. Louisville, Ky.: J. P. Morton, 1895.

Fitzpatrick, T. J. *Fitzpatrick's Rafinesque: A Sketch of His Life and Bibliography*. Weston, Mass: M&S Press, 1982.

Hance, Anthony M. "Rafinesque; the Great Naturalist." Paper read before Bucks County Historical Society, Langhorne, P., April 16, 1914. Pamphlet published 1916.

Herrick, Francis Hobart. *Audubon the Naturalist: A History of His Life and Time*. New York: Dover, 1968.

Jillson, Willard Rouse. *Some Kentucky Obliquities in Retrospect*. Frankfort, Ky.: Roberts Print, 1952.

Jordan, David Starr. "Rafinesque." *The Popular Science Monthly*, vol. XXIX, 1886.

Rafinesque, C. S. *A Life of Travels and Researches in North America and South Europe*. Printed for the author by F. Turner, Philadelphia, 1836.

Rafinesque, C. S. *The Pleasures and Duties of Wealth*. Printed for the Eleutherium of Knowledge, Philadelphia, 1840.

Chapter IV

Bernier, Olivier. *Louis XIV: A Royal Life*. New York: Doubleday, 1987.

Brocher, Louis, *A la cour de Louis XIV: Le rang et l'étiquette sous l'ancien régime*. Paris: F. Alcan, 1934.

Dangeau, Philippe de Courcillon. *Memoirs of the Court of France, from the year 1684 to the Year 1720*. Translated by John Davenport. London: H. Colburn, 1825.

Duchêne, Jacqueline. *Bussy-Rabutin*. Paris: Fayard, 1992.

Félibien, André. *Relation de la fête du dix-huit juillet mille six cent soixante-huit; Les divertissements de Versailles donnés par le Roi à toute sa cour au retour de la conquête de la Franche-Comté en l'année mille six cent soixante-quatorze*. Dédale: Maisonneuve et Larose, c. 1994.

Goldsmith, Elizabeth C. *Exclusive Conversations: The Art of Interaction in Seventeenth-Century France*. Philadelphia: University of Pennsylvania Press, 1988.

Les heures bourguignonnes du comte de Bussy-Rabutin. Autun: Musée Rolin, 1993.

Ojala, Jeanne A., and William T. Ojala. *Madame de Sévigné: A Seventeenth-Century Life*. New York: St. Martin's Press, 1990.

Rabutin, Roger de Bussy. *Correspondance de Roger de Rabutin, comte de Bussy*. Paris: Charpentier, 1858–1859.

Rabutin-Chantal, Marie de [Madame de Sévigné]. *Selected Letters*. Translated by Leonard Tancock. New York: Penguin, 1982.

Saint-Simon, Louis de Rouvroy de, *Memoirs*. Vol. I. Translated by Lucy Norton. London: Prion Books, 1999.

Chapter V

Calmette, Joseph. *The Golden Age of Burgundy: The Magnificent Dukes and Their Courts*. Translated by Doreen Weightman. New York: W. W. Norton, 1963.

Huizinga, Johan. *The Autumn of the Middle Ages*. Translated by Rodney J. Payton and Ulrich Mammitzsch. Chicago: University of Chicago Press, 1996.

La Marche, Oliver de. *Le chevalier délibéré (The Resolute Knight)*. Edited by Carleton W. Carroll; translated by Lois Hawley and Carleton W. Carroll. Tempe: Arizona Center for Medieval and Renaissance Studies, 1999.

La Marche, Olivier de. *Les mémoires de Messire Olivier de la Marche*. In *Nouvelle collection des mémoires pour servir à l'histoire de France depuis le XIIIe siècle jusqu'à la fin du XVIIIe*. Series 1, vol. 3. Lyon: Guyot, 1851.

Paston Letters and Papers of the Fifteenth Century. Edited by Norman Davis. Oxford: Clarendon Press, 1971–76.

Putnam, Ruth. *Charles the Bold, Last Duke of Burgundy, 1433–1477*. New York: G.P. Putnam, 1908.

Taillevent [Guillaume Tirel]. *The Viandier of Taillevent*. Edited by Terence Scully. Ottawa: University of Ottawa Press, 1988.

Weightman, Christine. *Margaret of York, Duchess of Burgundy, 1446–1503*. New York: St. Martin's Press, 1989.

Chapter VI

Allott, Stephen. *Alcuin of York: His Life and Letters*. York: William Sessions Ltd., 1974.

Asser, John. *Life of King Alfred*. Translated by Simon Keynes. New York: Penguin, 1983.

Bede. *A History of the English Church and People*. Translated by Leo Sherley-Price. New York: Penguin, 1983.

Beowulf. Translated by Seamus Heaney. New York: Farrar, Straus and Giroux, 2000.

Caesar, Julius. *Gallic War*. Translated by H. J. Edwards. Cambridge: Harvard University Press, 1997.

Davis, H. W. Carless. *Charlemagne, the Hero of Two Nations*. New York: Putnam, 1899.

Einhard. *The Life of Charlemagne*. Ann Arbor: University of Michigan Press, 1960.

Gregory of Tours. *The History of the Franks*. Translated by Lewis Thorpe. New York: Penguin, 1974.

Jordanes. *Origin and Deeds of the Goths*. Translated by Charles C. Mierow. Princeton: Princeton University Press, 1908.

Lacey, Robert, and Danny Danziger. *The Year 1000: What Life Was Like at the Turn of the First Millennium*. New York: Little, Brown, 1999.

Magennis, Hugh. *Anglo-Saxon Appetites: Food and Drink and Their Consumption in Old English and Related Literature*. Portland: Four Courts Press, 1999.

Monk of Saint Gall [Notker the Stammerer]. *Life of Charlemagne*. In *Two Lives of Charlemagne*. Translated by Lewis Thorpe. Baltimore: Penguin, 1969.

Nithard. *Nithard's Histories*. Translated by B. W. Scholz. Ann Arbor: University of Michigan Press, 1972.

Royal Frankish Annals. Translated by B. W. Scholz. Ann Arbor: University of Michigan Press, 1972.

Tacitus. *Germania*. Translated by M. Hutton et al. Cambridge: Harvard University Press, 1997.

Todd, Malcolm. *The Early Germans*. Cambridge: Blackwell, 1992.

Velleius Paterculus. *Historiae Romanae*. Translated by Frederick W. Shipley. Cambridge: Harvard University Press, 1924.

Voragine, Jacobus de. *The Golden Legend: Readings on the Saints*. Translated by W. R. Granger. Princeton: Princeton University Press, 1993.

Wade-Evans, A. W. *Nennius's "History of the Britons," together with "The Annals of the Britons," and "Court Pedigress of Hywel the Good," also "The Story of the Loss of Britain."* London: Society for Promoting Christian Knowledge, 1938.

Whitelock, Dorothy. *The Beginnings of English Society*. New York: Penguin, 1986.

Chapter VII

Apicius. *De re coquinaria*. Translated by Joseph Dommers Vehling. New York: Dover Publications, 1977.

Boëthius, Axel. *The Golden House of Nero: Some Aspects of Roman Architecture*. Ann Arbor: University of Michigan Press, 1960.

Corbett, Philip B. *Petronius*. New York: Twayne Pubs., 1970.

Iacopi, Irene. *Domus aurea*. Milan: Electa, 1999.

Macrobius. *Saturnalia*. Translated by Percival Vaughan Davies. New York: Columbia University Press, 1969.

Martial. *Epigrams*. Translated by D. R. Shackleton Bailey. Cambridge: Harvard University Press, 1993.

Petronius. *The Satyricon*. Translated by Paul Dinnage. London: Spearman & Calder, 1953.

Plutarch. "How to Tell a Flatterer from a Friend." In *Moralia*, Vol. I. Translated by Frank C. Babbitt. Cambridge: Harvard University Press, 1928.

Suetonius. *Lives of the Caesars*. Translated by Catherine Edwards. New York: Oxford University Press, 2000.

Tacitus. *The Annals of Imperial Rome*. Translated by Michael Grant. New York: Penguin, 1980.

Chapter VIII

Athenaeus of Naucratis. *The Deipnosophists*. Translated by Charles Burton Gulick. Cambridge: Harvard University Press, 1993.

Dalby, Andrew. *Siren Feasts: A History of Food and Gastronomy in Greece*. New York: Routledge, 1996.

Homer. *The Iliad*. Translated by Robert Fagles. New York: Penguin, 1990.

Homer. *The Odyssey*. Translated by Robert Fagles. New York: Penguin, 1999.

Ovid. *Metamorphoses*. Translated by Mary M. Innes. New York: Penguin, 1985.

Plato. *Symposium*. Translated by Christopher Gill. New York: Penguin, 1991.

Xenophon. *Symposium*. In *Works*, Vol. IV. Translated by O. J. Todd. Cambridge: Harvard University Press, 1968.

A NOTE ON THE AUTHOR

Jesse Browner was born and lives in New York City. He is the author of two novels, *Conglomeros* and *Turnaway*, and has translated works by Cocteau, Rilke, Eluard, and others.

A NOTE ON THE TYPE

Guardi was designed by Reinhard Haus of Linotype in 1987. It was named after the Guardi brothers, Gianantonio and Francesco, the last famous artists from the Renaissance Venetian school of painting. It is based on the Venetian text styles of the fifteenth century. The influence of characters originally written with a feather can be seen in many aspects of this modern alphabet.